M000268234

JAKE HANNA

to Nelson,
Thanks for
suggesting Gary
Giddins to me.
He made me
realize this should
be a book.
Cheers,
Mia

THE RHYTHM
AND WiT
OF A
SWINGING
JAZZ
DRUMMER

MARIA S. JUDGE

PRAISE FOR MARIA JUDGE'S
JAKE HANNA: THE RHYTHM AND WIT OF A SWINGING JAZZ DRUMMER

"This book is full of humor, honesty and wisdom — three things that were always present in Jake Hanna as a person, and always in his music!"

—*Howard Alden*, *Jazz guitarist*

"Our fathers would have loved this book. I know that my dad [jazz critic] Leonard Feather admired Jake personally and professionally and wrote about him in many different publications. Before my dad, [drummer] Lloyd Morales went on to perform with Les Brown, Lainie Kazan and Mitzi Gaynor, he was Jake's sergeant during his Air Force basic training and taught him to read music so he could get into the band."

—*Lorraine Feather* (singer, lyricist, songwriter) and *Tony Morales* (drummer)

"In my childhood days in Italy I always admired Jake Hanna's artistry on records. Years later, when I moved to the US to pursue my dream, I had the incredible opportunity to meet him. I was so thrilled when he agreed to play with me. It was the start of a beautiful musical and personal friendship that led us to make music together all over the world. I will always cherish the time I spent with Jake on and off stage ... an amazing lesson in musicality, artistry, wit and most of all, human feeling. The stories in this book will help to keep his memory alive. Swing on, Jake!"

—*Roberta Gambarini*, *Jazz vocalist and recording artist*

"Jake Hanna's niece, Maria Judge, has put together a wonderful collection of stories and anecdotes to tell Jake's story in a highly readable way. She relates his life and career through recollections from family members, long time friends and fellow musicians, along with material from Jake himself. There are contributions and quotes from Jim Hall, Lew Tabackin, and fellow drummers like Jeff Hamilton and Butch Miles. Let's thank the author for giving another part of the history of this music we love called jazz."

—*Eric Jackson*, *Host of "Jazz on WGBH with Eric Jackson"*

"Jake Hanna was one of the hardest swinging drummers I ever heard, and he achieved it on a modest kit, with great skill and apparent nonchalance. I was privileged to introduce broadcasts of Jake and his music for the BBC, which gave me the chance to interview him at length. There was never enough time for all that Jake had to say about his amazing career and experiences, but this book draws as much as possible about him together in one place, and for those of us who loved him and his music, offers answers to the questions we never had time to ask."

—*Alyn Shipton*, *Presenter, BBC Radio 3, London*

"Jake Hanna was a good friend to my father and grandfather, Armand and Avedis, and to many of us at the Zildjian Company. Those people not fortunate enough to have known Jake personally will be grateful for this book, which brings to life his wonderful talent, his inimitable sense of humor, and his larger than life personality."

—*Craigie Zildjian*, *CEO, Avedis Zildjian Company*

This book is dedicated to
Denisa Heitman Hanna,
who doted on, cared for, tended to and loved Jake
for 34 adventure-filled years.

The Hanna siblings—Eleanor, Billy, Jake and Mary—all memorable,
all musical, always singing, almost always swinging.

Danny Judge, Shirley Ray Judge and Marilyn Lahmer Judge—
music lovers all.

Published by
Meredith Music Publications
a division of G.W. Music, Inc.
4899 Lerch Creek Ct., Galesville, MD 20765
http://www.meredithmusic.com

MEREDITH MUSIC PUBLICATIONS and its stylized double M logo are trademarks of
MEREDITH MUSIC PUBLICATIONS, a division of G.W. Music, Inc.

Cover and text design: Shawn Girsberger

Cover photo: Al White

International Standard Book Number: 978-1-57463-192-0
Cataloging-in-Publication Data is on file with the Library of Congress.
Library of Congress Control Number: 2012944306
Printed and bound in U.S.A.

Contents

ACKNOWLEDGEMENTS

Nancy Arnison and I coached each other via daily phone calls for two years to finish writing my book and her dissertation. We completed both projects within weeks of each other.

Lynette Benton was the best literary partner a two-person writing group could have. She encouraged, inspired, prodded, questioned and edited me for more than a year and made me stick to my schedule. Actually she had me *make* the schedule first and *then* stick to it.

Larry Bushey, Jake's high school classmate and yearbook editor, loaned me his Dorchester High School yearbook and I didn't return it for two years. Thank you for your patience Larry.

Sue Buzzard was a fine Research Assistant who wove together Jake's discography, edited the manuscript and helped with promotion.

Carol Calato, Bill Clancy, Chip Deffaa, John King, Marian McPartland, Bob Rusch and John Tumpack very kindly allowed me to use their previously published materials.

Vladimir Florentino and Juan Abenza were invaluable technological resources.

Helena Halperin and Elaine Gottlieb were there before the beginning.

Mike Hegarty gave me access to some great historical information about Berklee during Jake's student days.

Aidan Judge and Christina Belforti were a big help researching jazz radio stations.

Brigid, Rory and Eleanor Judge, Mary Howard and Denisa Hanna read drafts of the manuscript and provided useful feedback and fact-checking.

Al Julian knew everyone and had their phone numbers. I don't know how I could have written this book without his prodigious memory, extensive network and collection of books, pictures and musical references.

My fellow "Chicks Who Write," especially Betsy Lawson, Katherine Waters Clark, Jane Whitehead, Janet Mendelsohn and Stephanie Schorow, were great supporters and encouragers.

Laurinda Bedingfeld and I shared many writing sessions at True Grounds Coffee Shop, The Diesel Café, and Zing Café at Porter Square Books. My hometown Medford Public Library, which I patronize weekly, has lots of literary resources and convenient quiet spaces. Marblehead's Abbot Public Library and Muffin Shop hosted me for long writing sessions. My Branca, Judge and Vogt cousins provided wonderful creative space and good company at their Pocasset cottages, as did the Mahers in GIW.

Nancy Mulvihill, Michael Steinman, Jim Szantor and Jeri Zeder were invaluable editors who helped to make the prose flow, provided extensive feedback, and collectively found thousands of missing commas and waylaid quotation marks. They ensured that a book about a perfectionist like Jake didn't take shortcuts or get sloppy because the author forgot the basics of grammar and punctuation.

Brian Peerless was a great UK resource and tracked down every reference request I sent him.

Garwood Whaley of Meredith Music Publications took a chance on this book, for which I'm very grateful.

PRELUDE

Jake Hanna was chosen Jazz Legend of the 2010 San Diego Jazz Party. His death one week before the event cast a pall upon the proceedings, particularly since most of the performers and many of the attendees were longtime friends and fans. Throughout the weekend the Jake stories flew through the air. Some we'd heard before, others were new. Some were recent, others related events that happened 40 years earlier but the raconteurs recalled them in great detail, like Ed Polcer's story about Jake and the Hell's Angels who were trying to ruin his club.

I listened in amazement and thought *we need to save these stories while we still remember them, before the storytellers are gone.*

Then I realized I was the one who would have to do this.

As Jake's niece, I was fortunate to have heard his music and his stories for decades. I knew he was a great musician—you had to be *very* good to count Bing Crosby, Count Basie, Charlie Watts AND Joe DiMaggio among your fans—and it was a treat to hear him play, whether at family weddings and reunions with old friends, or at the Rainbow Room in Rockefeller Center.

For years he was just plain Uncle Jake, a regular guy who came to visit, slept in the bottom bunk bed in my brothers' room, wore black silk shoes (maybe that wasn't so 'plain'), and sat at the dining room table with my mother, reminiscing about the old neighborhood and their childhood friends. He had circled the world during his seven decades as a musician, but never forgot his high school classmates or his Air Force band mates, or the guys he hung out with on the courthouse wall. And they never forgot him.

As I got older I developed an appreciation for just how funny he was and how often his witty remarks were repeated, though most people couldn't master his deadpan delivery, his Baw-stun accent or his split second timing. How could they. There was only one Jake.

In the ancient Celtic culture of his ancestors, Jake may have been fulfilling the role of the shanachie, the traditional Irish storytellers, who sometimes traveled from one community to another, exchanging their creativity for food and temporary shelter. So it seemed appropriate to recount Jake's life through the stories he told and that others told about him. Occasionally I heard several versions of the same story but I included all variations, as I imagine the shanachies did themselves.

Jake had many advantages not always available to young musicians: an older brother who was a great drummer; a drum and bugle corps devoted to developing young talent; a war that took many professional musicians out of town and gave underage musicians access to the kinds of gigs they wouldn't normally get as well as make connections in the musical world; a city—Boston—where jazz was popular, plentiful and accessible; a period of service in the military that afforded him the time to perfect his skills; an academic institution focused on the needs of professional drummers; lots of opportunities to work with exceptionally talented musicians; and a place—New York—and era—the 1960s—where he could sit in with the best musicians of the day. So when he had an opportunity to help someone he thought had great potential, he was always willing to lend a hand.

Many of those he helped have lent a hand here by sharing their stories. Collecting them has been quite an experience, bittersweet because it is a reminder that he is gone, yet richly rewarding, as I've spent hundreds of delightful and often hilarious hours talking to friends and fans and recording their memories of him.

Here are some of those memories.

Maria Judge

Opening Bars

I became aware of Jake when I was playing at Storyville in Boston, and asked him to join my group in 1959, which he did shortly thereafter. The enjoyment of this period was interrupted only once, when Jake (who became well known for giving little or no notice when he decided to leave a band), elected to go back to Boston to work with the Herb Pomeroy Band. Being the diplomat he was, he handed me his notice—and a parting gift of a Waring Blender—simultaneously. He returned after a few weeks … to join me at the Hickory House where, with Ben Tucker on bass, we spend one of the swing-ingest summers I have ever known. He worked with me for two years and then moved on. Later, he and I were on several recording dates together for Concord Jazz, and it was always a kick to play with him.

There was an easy flow, a logical methodical purpose to everything Jake did. He followed established patterns set down by Dave Tough and Don Lamond and drew inspiration from them and from his idols Jo Jones and Buddy Rich, not consciously copying them, but nevertheless revealing their influence while adding his own unique personality, imagination and humor. He was a pleasure to watch; there was no wasted motion, yet he was a flamboyant performer who did everything with a flourish and a jaunty good-natured air. He used his technique logically—no unnecessary pyro-technics—and he had the good judgment and the power necessary to hold and control the rhythm at all times.

Jake was almost without peer in his particular field as a big band drummer, studio musician, accompanist, and a small group player in trios, quartets and quintet. He was a musician in the true sense, totally involved with playing, discussing music and listening to it, and he was one of the most completely cheerful people one could meet. Though he affected a bluff air and joking irrev-erent attitude toward most things, he was still sincere, dedicated and honest.

Jake's zeal for playing remained strong, as did his philosophy of life, characteristically humorous and simple: "Life is a fight and naturally I don't want to get wasted. So I take things as they come. Nice and easy."

Marian McPartland, from "All in Good Time"

Born on Beaumont Street

'Sunny Skies Forecast for the Easter Parade' read the teaser above the front page headline of the *Boston Traveler* of Saturday, April 4, 1931. Temperatures were expected to be in the mid-40s on Easter Sunday, and churchgoers were promised moderate northwest winds as they strolled the streets of Boston in their Easter finery.

Jim Hanna couldn't have known, as he was setting the type for that issue of the newspaper, that it would commemorate the birth date of his third son. But shortly before he got home that morning from his night shift at the newspaper, John Edwin Hanna was born in the second floor flat at 65 Beaumont Street in Dorchester, Massachusetts. He joined his two surviving siblings, seven-year-old Billy and eight-and-a-half year old Eleanor. His oldest brother James Jr., known as Buddy, had died of pneumonia when he was two years old, just a few months after Eleanor was born.

Jim Hanna had been working in the newspaper business for more than twenty years by the time Jake was born. He was born and raised 60 miles away in the central Massachusetts town of Fitchburg. His father, James, was a coal merchant, so successful and with such a high standing in the community that when the Hanna family went to Sunday Mass, Jim and his brother Paul were nattily attired in top hats. James hailed from Belfast, Northern Ireland, but came to the United States when he was twelve. He inherited the business from his own father, and probably hoped to pass it on to his sons. But James and his wife died when their five children were still young and Jim quit school after his sophomore year to work as an errand boy at the Fitchburg Sentinel, where he eventually learned the printer's trade.

The paper that the Sentinel was printed on may very well have been made by Jake's maternal grandfather. William Nichols was a hobo papermaker who traveled the country before landing in Fitchburg in 1894, where he was hired by the Crocker Burbank Paper Mills. He worked there for the next thirty years, except for the seven or eight times when the wanderlust overtook him and he quit his job and left town[1]. He always returned and must have been a very good papermaker since Crocker Burbank always gave him back his job.

William's daughter Ella, Jake's mother, was a studious girl who wanted to go to Teachers College when she graduated from high school. But despite her father's propensity to quit his jobs when the spirit moved him, he decided she should develop a solid work ethic. He told her she'd had enough studying and it was time to go to work. She got a job as secretary to the Chief of Police in Fitchburg where she worked until she married Jim Hanna in 1919.

The following stories come from Jake's sisters and Dorchester friends.

———

My father's cousins from Fitchburg came to visit us one Friday evening. One of them was a chatty woman who didn't notice my mother's increasing discomfort over the course of the evening. It was almost midnight by the time they left, and shortly after that Mama, who was nine months pregnant, realized she had gone into labor. My father was at work, so she called the doctor and told him she couldn't get to the hospital. He lived nearby, so he told her he would come right away. At that point she had such a bad contraction she grabbed hold of the radiator and almost pulled it out of

---

1 Jake may have inherited a bit of his grandfather's wanderlust.

the floor. She finally got herself into bed and Jake was born a few minutes later. He beat the doctor who arrived shortly afterwards and began to take care of things.

My father arrived home just then.

"Jim, get something to put the baby in," ordered the doctor, who was holding the newborn and looking around for a place to put him. Pa left the room and reappeared a minute later with a laundry basket. This wasn't exactly what the doctor had in mind.

"Get something to wrap him in," he told Pa, who returned with an army blanket, his own army blanket that he brought back from the war. It was an ugly shade of brown and very rough.[2]

Billy and I slept in a bedroom off the front hall, right across from the dining room. A noise woke me up so I got out of bed and went into the dining room where my father was having breakfast. There was a clothes basket on the floor.

"What's that doing there," I asked Pa.

"That's your brother," he told me.

I looked in the basket and saw a tiny baby lying there.

Eleanor Hanna Judge

He was named John Edwin Hanna, but nicknamed Jake after my father's uncle Walter who was known as Jake.

Mary Hanna Howard

We always called him Johnny at home. He didn't get the nick-name Jake until he was in high school. His friends started calling him "Jake the flake," not because he was flaky, but after Corn Flakes, since they used to call people 'corny.' He wasn't named after Uncle Walter.[3]

Eleanor Hanna Judge

---

2   Jim Hanna's resourcefulness may explain where Jake got his improvisational skills, as well as his propensity for working the night shift.

3   Apparently Jake wasn't the only one who occasionally remembered more than one version of the same story.

My mother had just ordered the phone a few months earlier, specifically so Pa could call her if he was going to be late from work. Since he often returned home by way of the Ashmont Grille or the Bamboo Bar at the Hotel Avery, being late was a common occurrence, but he never once called her. She finally returned it to the phone company, although luckily not until after the night Jake was born.

Eleanor Hanna Judge

How ironic that the child destined to make the world come alive with the sound of his drums began with an appeal for silence. I recall an article that young Eleanor Hanna wrote for the Woodrow Wilson School magazine in which she reported that her young brother's first words were "Shhhh, daddy's sleeping."

Robert Louis Sheehan

One day when Jake was about three years old my mother got him dressed up to go someplace special. He had on a white suit with a little bow tie and shorts and he was very neat and clean. She put him out on the front porch with careful instructions to stay there and not get dirty. Then she went inside to get ready herself.

A few minutes later there was a knock on the door and lady stood there holding Jake by the hand.

"Is this your son?" she asked my mother.

"Yes, what happened?" Mama wondered.

"I saw him walking down Westmoreland Street with one foot on the sidewalk and one foot in the gutter and he was hopping along."

"What are you doing, little boy," I asked him.

"Lady," he said, staring up at me, "I'm a ragman's horse."[4]

Eleanor Hanna Judge

---

4 The ragman came around the neighborhood often in his horse-drawn cart to collect rags. Jake must have admired his horse.

When I was in the third grade my mother had to go into the hospital for surgery. She didn't want Jake and me to be home by ourselves after school, so she arranged for our next door neighbor to keep an eye on us. I had a better idea and suggested that Jake take me to the movies. Papa thought that was a good idea too, so Jake took me to the Uphams Corner Cinema to see *Man Hunt.* We liked it so much we went back to see it three days in a row.[5]

Mary Hanna Howard

Jake came down with scarlet fever when he was three and our family had to be quarantined. Billy and I had to stay home from school for six weeks. Then Mary got it and we were quarantined again.

Eleanor Hanna Judge

5 *Man Hunt* starred Walter Pidgeon as an English big-game hunter arrested near Berchtesgaden for aiming his rifle at Adolf Hitler. Joan Bennett played the Cockney streetwalker with a heart of gold who helps him as he is chased across Europe by villainous Nazis, led by George Sanders, who traps him in a cave and tosses in the arrow-shaped brooch he gave to Bennett. Pidgeon realizes Sanders has killed her, so he makes an arrow with the brooch and shoots Sanders in the head. It did not seem suitable viewing for third and fourth graders.

2

OFD—Originally From Dorchester

*B*uddy and Eleanor Hanna were both born in a three-decker on Lonsdale Street, but after Buddy's death, Ella felt the apartment held too many memories of her little boy, so they moved to Beaumont Street. Billy and Jake were born there and the following year they moved to a two-family house at 74 Elmer Road. A year later they moved to another two-family at 72 Westmoreland Street, and a 1937 move took them to yet another two-family on Minot Street. Despite all these moves, the family never went far since Beaumont, Elmer, Westmoreland and Minot Streets were all within one block of each other.

The streets were also in St. Brendan's Parish, which was an important distinction, because parishes helped to define neighborhoods in those days. When asked where you lived, people were as likely to respond with a parish name as they were with a street name. Some of their friends who weren't even Catholic used to say they lived in St. Brendan's since that seemed easier for people to understand.

The Hanna family's frequent moves were often due to a need to stay one jump ahead of the landlord, a fairly common practice in Depression-era Dorchester. Dorchester had been settled in 1630 by immigrants from Plymouth, England and by 1870, when it was annexed to Boston, the population had grown to 12,000. When Jake was born there were more than 150,000 people living in the thousands of three-deckers that had sprung up around town.

The three-deckers were solid housing built to give families the benefit of suburban life while living close to city jobs. The three family houses derived their names from the three-story rear porches that appeared to be stacked one on top of the other. They were built along the streetcar line to make it easy for the men to travel into downtown Boston for work. Boston was among the first cities in the world to have a complete metropolitan streetcar system and its expansion into Dorchester, combined with the growth of housing, made Dorchester affordable to a commuting lower middle class like the Hannas.

Jim Hanna was a member of the powerful International Typographical Union, which provided its members with the best working conditions in the American publishing industry, a 40-hour work week and a standard wage scale for all printers in the city. When many of his friends were out of work during the Depression, he always had a job. The Hanna family owed a debt of gratitude to his union friends who went to bat for him several times when his drinking became a problem and convinced the bosses to keep him on. He was a talented worker, though, and had the particular skill required for setting up the stock market pages in their complicated columnar format. He worked a variety of shifts, starting with 5 p.m. to 1 or 2 a.m., because the newspaper often came out as early as 3 each morning. Later he transferred over to the "lobster shift," which began around 5 a.m. and put out the afternoon and evening paper.

Jim and Ella Hanna were proud of their children and expected them to work hard and succeed. Jim encouraged his sons in their musical pursuits. Both boys began playing the drums in the Saint Brendan's Drum and Bugle Corps when they turned seven, Billy in 1931 and Jake in 1938. As the boys got older and more interested in drumming, they wanted to see live music for themselves. Jim got tickets through the newspaper to the downtown theaters, and Jake would take the streetcar downtown to spend an entire afternoon and evening listening to big bands. This occasionally required him skipping school, but he managed to get away with it.

Jake was ten years old when World War II broke out, and within a few years, he and Billy were hanging around and playing at the downtown clubs and theatres. During the war years there was a shortage of musicians—many of them were in the service—so two young drummers who could keep the beat were in demand. Jake was thirteen and looked even younger, but he was already taller than Billy, who had scoliosis and never grew more than five feet tall.

Jake's and Billy's gigs stopped when the professional musicians returned from the war.

The following stories come from Jake's family, Dorchester friends and from his own interviews.

I started hitting the drums at CYO, Catholic Youth Organization. I heard the church band, and I wanted to play in it. I started playing when I was five or six — a little peewee drum and bugle. The music was as simple as you can get: "Our Director," stuff like that. My brother — he was about five years older than me — played in the regular band, with trombone and clarinets, up in front of us. That was when we were little kids in the '30s. And I just kept playing a little. I didn't really follow music. I just played ball a lot. I never studied music.

Jake Hanna, as told to Chip Deffaa

I used to go visit my classmate Mary Hanna at her house on Minot Street and I would see her brother Jake playing the drums in the big square lobby area just inside their front door. He always seemed to be there banging on the drums.

Joan Filippone

My parents couldn't afford to buy drums for Billy and Jake, so they practiced on anything — and everything — they could find. One of their favorite places to practice in the house was on my mother's sewing machine case. The two of them practiced so much that they wore off the finish.

Mary Hanna Howard

I could hear Jake and Billy playing the drums in their bedroom on Washington Street. They moved the sewing machine in there and played music on the record player while they drummed along.

Ruth Nutting

My brother stole my drumsticks and had the career that should have been mine.

Billy Hanna

Why did I want to play the drums? I had no choice. My brother played the drums, my father played the drums. When the war started this guy left his drums at our house, one of the last drum sets made with metal parts; after that, they were made with wooden parts. It was a 32-inch bass drum, and my brother was only five feet tall but he played the shit out of it. I listened to my brother playing. He had a real hot beat. I wanted to be Gene Krupa, who else?

Jake Hanna as told to Rory Judge

When I was seven we moved from Minot Street to Washington Street but the cat didn't follow us. I kept telling my mother that she needed to go back for it, and finally she told us to get it ourselves. So Jake and I found a container and lugged it the two miles back to our old house. We finally found the cat, put it in the container, closed the cover and then began the return trip. It was so much heavier with the cat in it, and Jake and I fought all the way home. I said he was walking too fast and he said I was walking too slowly and we grumbled at each other the entire walk. Even though he liked cats I think he just didn't want to do this errand.

Mary Hanna Howard

Our house at 430 Washington Street was three doors down from a park called Mother's Rest[6], though not many mothers found the neighborhood restful after we moved in. A very patient, kind family lived on the second floor, and I think they were partly responsible for Jake's musical success because they never complained about his drumming. Then a pediatrician moved onto the first floor and set up his office on one side of the flat. The trolley stopped right in front of our house and the passengers would peer through the windows at the baby carriages lined up on the front walkway, then stare up at the third floor where the sounds of beating drums echoed around the neighborhood. I can only imagine what they thought was going on in that house.

Mary Hanna Howard

The Hanna family may have thought we never complained, but I can't count the times I stood on my bed and pounded on the ceiling with a broom to get them to stop that noise. But of course Jake and Billy couldn't hear me through their drumming.

Cheryl McManus

When Jake was in the sixth grade my mother got a note from his teacher, informing her that he was a very bright student and recommending he transfer to Boston Latin School. My mother didn't think that was a good idea and kept him at the Woodrow Wilson School. Apparently Mama knew her son better than his teachers did because at the end of that year Jake was held back and had to repeat the sixth grade.

Mary Hanna Howard

---

6 Edwin Booth, the great 19th century actor, rented the house next door to Mother's Rest for a few months in 1862 and 1863. Unfortunately, neither he nor his mother got much rest two years later when his brother John Wilkes assassinated Abraham Lincoln.

When I was in the sixth grade my mother thought I should transfer to Girl's Latin School. She spoke to my teacher who told her I was too young to be traveling into Boston by myself and I would do just as well at the Woodrow Wilson. So I stayed there and did just fine. She must have had that incident in mind nine years later when Jake's teacher suggested he transfer.

Eleanor Hanna Judge

I forgot to bring my lunch to school one morning, so when Jake left the house a few minutes after I did, my mother told him to bring it to me. He resented the chore. My teacher, Miss Bergamini, had just started class when there was a knock on the door of my seventh grade homeroom. She called out 'come in,' and the door opened. Jake shuffled across the floor, slapped the bag down on her desk and told her "this is my sister's."

"And who is your sister?" asked Miss Bergamini, glaring at him.

"Mary Hanna," he mumbled, then slouched his way back out.

Miss Bergamini stared at me for a long minute, then ordered the class to sit still and told me to stand up.

"Were you brought up in a barn?!?" she thundered.

I just stared at her. She was appropriately named because she was a "meany." It was a badge of honor to be called out by her, so I knew the rest of the class was rooting for me.

"What kind of a brother would enter a classroom like that," she continued.

I was mad at Jake so when I got home I complained to my mother.

"Jake was mean to me today. I almost got in trouble and it wasn't my fault," I told her.

"Next time don't forget your lunch," said Mama.

Mary Hanna Howard

My brother showed me basically what to do as a drummer. I do basically the same thing today, without any variation. I was very lucky. When I was about 11 or 12, he showed me the right way to play the cymbal beat ... And it was ingrained. I says, "Oh, that's the way it goes. I didn't know it could go stiff or loose or bad." He showed me the exact right way to do it....

Jake Hanna, as told to Chip Deffaa

Oh, Jake was a character. You never knew what would come out of his mouth.

Dave Kenney

He was serious in class, though. He was a hard worker.

Charlie Delaney

I used to see Jake in the lunchroom playing on the table. If he didn't have his drumsticks he'd just use his hands.

Jim Shea

Jake could play the dashboard too. He'd sit in the front set of your car and beat out rhythms on the dashboard.

Fran Shaw

I sat next to Jake in one of our classes. He'd drum on his desk with a pencil and a ruler. One day the teacher said to him, "You're going to grow up to be a bum!"

Paul Kenney

I saw Jake and Paul Fitzpatrick one day riding from the subway from Ashmont to Harvard. They were standing up, holding onto the white porcelain handles and snapping them back and forth in a drum-like rhythm.

Jack O'Callaghan

Jake Hanna was four years older than me and was friends with my brother Pierce, who he called Specs, and who we called Jake. We lived on Washington Street on the corner of West Tremlett, two blocks away from the Dorchester District Courthouse. Pierce and his friends used to meet up there to play touch football. The courthouse was surrounded by a granite wall about two feet high that the guys used to sit on. When Jake sat there he'd straddle the wall and hit on it with his drumsticks.

My mother and I were walking past the courthouse one day when we saw Jake playing the wall.

"Is that all you have to do?" my mother asked him. "Just beat those sticks?"

"Hi, Mrs. McCarthy," said Jake. "Someday they're going to pay me to beat these sticks."

Jim McCarthy

From 8th grade on we used to go to dances on Friday and Saturday nights, first at the Community Center and later at St. Matthews Church Hall. Jake played there with a trio of musicians. I remember two of the songs they played: "Five Minutes More," and "Good Night Sweetheart." When you heard them you knew it was time to go home.

Joan Filippone

Jake was a funny guy in high school. He was part of the crowd that didn't have dates on Sunday nights, so those guys would congregate at Rogers Ice Cream Shop, across from the Codman Square Theatre, where they could keep an eye out for the guys who had dates. The guys with dates knew they were across the street so they'd try to sneak the girls in before we could see them, but the ticket booth was practically on the street so we always caught them. When we saw them walk up to the ticket counter, we'd holler across the street "two please" before they could even place their ticket order. Jake and Herb Ingraham led the chant, rubbing it in a bit because those guys had dates and we didn't. We'd go in later but of course we only bought one ticket.

Eddie Miller

Drums, I got influenced by John Philip Sousa ... still am. That whole phrasing he does, the musicality and the harmonies. John Philip Sousa was one of the greatest ever. And that's what influenced me gettin' into music. And the bands. I'd go hear those bands, I had a great opportunity, go to the theaters, sit there...the hell with school. Truant officers used to come after me.

Jake Hanna, Cadence interview

When I served in the WAVES[7] during World War II, I met an Army officer who worked down the hall. Sherm Feller[8] was assigned to Special Services which handled entertainment. Before joining he used to have a radio show called Club Midnight where he interviewed performers after they finished their gigs at the downtown theatres and nightclubs. So he got to know lots of people in the music business. I think Jake must have met him when Sherm came to the house and of course he was very interested to hear all his stories about the people he'd interviewed on his show. He started hanging around clubs where Sherm was working and eventually Sherm started giving him tickets to different clubs where he heard some of the musicians he came to admire and, in some cases, play with later.

Eleanor Hanna Judge

A guy who used to go out with my sister really got me going

---

7   The acronym for the women's division of the U.S. Navy known as "Women Accepted for Volunteer Emergency Service."

8   Sherm Feller was also a talented composer who later became the "Voice of the Red Sox," serving as the public address announcer for the Boston Red Sox at Fenway Park for 26 years, which also endeared him to sports-loving Jake.

as a musician. He'd give me tickets to go see Benny Goodman and those guys during the war. There weren't many guys around in the bands (they were in the service).

Well, during the war, anybody could work. I worked when I was 13. They didn't care how old you were; they had to have somebody, man. People didn't want to dance to records. They wanted live bands: 13-, 14-piece bands. To play in a big band now is a luxury, a unique event. In those days, there were over a thousand bands working, especially after the war. Anybody could work then; I don't care how old you were. My brother was only about five feet tall and he worked all the time, underage, those real bad bars. And I was able to work all those joints, too, for $9 a night.

Jake Hanna as told to Chip Deffaa

The RKO in downtown Boston is where I got my musical education. All I had to pay was thirty-five cents to get in and I had a free pass to go backstage from my father's newspaper. I saw a lot of great drummers. There was Buddy Schutz with Jimmy Dorsey and Buddy Rich with Tommy Dorsey. Woody Herman appeared a lot with Don Lamond. Count Basie, Benny Goodman, Lionel Hampton, Louie Prima, they all played there. My favorite act was the Mills Brothers. They were the best of all the vocal groups.

Jake Hanna as told to John Tumpak

The Boston music scene was busy during the war years and the RKO Theatre was one of the most important places in big band Boston. It seated 2,900 people, and every Thursday a new band would come in and work for a week. A typical show would have an opening act — a juggler, or contortionist, or comedian, or a dog act — followed by the musical talent — maybe a local singer — then they'd show a movie, and finally, the feature attraction. The guys in the pit band had to play for everyone. The bands did four or five shows a day and night. People worked all kinds of schedules — defense workers got off at midnight — and were looking for entertainment after a long shift. The key to getting on a band was that you had to read anything and play it. Sunday afternoons there was a jam session and anyone who'd been playing in town would get to play.

Richard Vacca

The main guy who was a big influence on me was a friend of Ruby Braff's named Mel Braverman. He used to play Count Basie records for me, set the drums up, told me to lighten up on the foot — I used to play the bass drum very heavy — and showed me how to get a nice sound out of the hi-hat. He told me to listen to that Jo Jones sound, to imitate it. That's how I learned how to play. Shelley Manne told me that's how he learned too, from Jo Jones records.

Jake Hanna BBC interview

Jake marched in the School Boy Parades every year. We all did, it was required. You got one point a year and you needed four points to graduate from high school. We wore uniforms and practiced regularly. The parade route went all around Boston and the crowds cheered and the officials came out and it was really a big deal. They taught us how to march pretty well though, so we had an advantage when we went into the service a few years later.

Dave Kenney and Charlie Delaney

One night in 1947, shortly after I got out of the WAVES, a friend took me down to Nantasket Beach to hear Jake play at the Hotel Pemberton. It was located on a point at the far end of the town of Hull and was surrounded by water on three sides. Jake was only about 16 and it was a pretty fancy place for him to be playing.

Twelve years later they tore down the Hotel Pemberton and built a high school there.

A few years after that my husband and I moved to that town and eventually all nine of our children graduated from Hull High School.

Eleanor Hanna Judge

During the summer of 1948 a bunch of us had just gotten out of the service and we used to hang out at Malibu Beach in Dorchester. Jake was there all the time beating with his drumsticks. He'd beat on the rocks, on our heads, on anything and everything.

John Ratto

On graduation day in 1949, Jake got the biggest hand of anyone in the graduating class as he walked across the stage.

He came back down and I said to him "Jake, your fly is down."

"Gee, can you stand in front of me?" he asked.

Charlie Delaney

I was visiting Jake in Los Angeles about 30 years later and asked "Jake, do you remember Charlie Delaney?"

"Yeah," he said. "He's the guy who told me my fly was down on graduation day."

Fran Shaw

Everybody talks about what a great guy Jake was, but I didn't like him. In 1950 I bought a 1949 Ford Convertible. It was silver blue with a white top and twin spotlight. I thought I was the cat's meow driving that around. Each time Jake went by he pounded on the car with his drumsticks and drove me crazy.

We reconciled though and he loaned me his suit coat for my senior yearbook picture.

Jim Bono

Jake got a job at a little restaurant near Neponset Circle after he graduated from high school. He still didn't own any drums so he decided it was time to buy a set. He made arrangements to buy a set on credit, and then asked my mother if she could guarantee it. She said no, she couldn't afford to do that, and if he couldn't pay she would get stuck with the $100 bill.

My brother Billy said he would guarantee it, so he signed the agreement.

Jake played there one night and then the restaurant burned down.

Billy got stuck with the $100 loan.

About twenty five years later, Jake took Billy on a cruise that he was playing. He told him he was finally paying him back for the drums.

Mary Hanna Howard

Mary Hanna and I worked together at the Army Base in South Boston. I lived in the South End and when I went to visit her in Dorchester at her family's three-decker, I felt like I was going to the country because her neighborhood had trees and mine had concrete. I never saw her brother Jake during my visits, but I heard him banging away on the drums in his room.

The first time I saw him play was at a hotel lounge in Copley Square where he was with a trio. We sat at a little round table and I remember thinking, "Oh my gosh, I know somebody famous," because I figured if he was good enough to play in a hotel he *must* be famous!

Delores Mello

Jake stayed on for a "PG," a post graduate year, after he graduated from Dorchester High School for Boys. It was a popular thing for students to do at the time, especially if they were a bit young and unsure about what they wanted to do next. Even though Jake had repeated sixth grade he was only eighteen when he graduated, so it made sense for him to stay on. He didn't finish the whole year because he went into the Air Force the following March.

Eleanor Hanna Judge

The Korean War broke out in June. Jake may have decided to enlist early, and in the Air Force, because even though you had to stay for a longer period of time — 3 or 4 years — you got to pick what you wanted to do and you wouldn't necessarily be sent over-seas, like the rest of us who waited a few more months. Jake must have figured he could get in the band.

Dave Kenney

Jake and the Hannas

Eleanor Hanna Judge

I was eight-and-a-half-years-old when my brother Jake was born, sixteen-years-old when he started playing the drums, and I joined the WAVES when he was twelve. My brother Billy was two years younger than I and Mary was two years younger than Jake, so there was a seven-year gap between the two older and two younger children in my family. My memories of Jake as a child and young man are sometimes a bit vague because he was so much younger and I wasn't always aware of what he was doing. And the four of us usually went about our own business and didn't pay that much attention to each other. One afternoon we came home from school to find my mother playing bridge with some friends. One of the women looked us over as we arrived, one at a time, and finally said to Mama, "Do you have a different husband for every one of these kids? None of them looks alike and none of them acts alike."

My parents were high school sweethearts in Fitchburg and married when they were in their twenties. They were very sociable people, outgoing and friendly. Pa was a great storyteller and could be quite charming as long as he wasn't drinking. He didn't drink when he was young. Mama said he couldn't drink, alcohol used to make him turn green. "Later," she added dryly, "He managed to overcome it."

I was close to my father. Mama said "he really likes his kids." And he liked other kids too, he got a big kick out of children. Of course he wasn't really responsible for any of them, and not even for us when he needed to be. My mother had nervous breakdowns and was hospitalized several times over a period of about twenty five years. Her first breakdown happened after Buddy was born. I don't know if it was some kind of post-partum depression, or if my father's disposition was starting to show, but she would have them every three or four years. The summers were hard on her with the heat, and with all of us home from school. So she'd go off to the hospital and a relative or friend would come to stay with us and after a week or two she would come home and we'd resume our routine.

Jake was born when we lived on Beaumont Street in St. Brendan's Parish. The church was still under construction and wouldn't open for another two years, so he was baptized in the Granite Avenue Garage, on the corner of Gallivan Boulevard, half a mile away from our house. The St. Brendan's Drum and Bugle Corps was founded the year Jake was born. Billy was seven by then and my father encouraged him to join the first group of band members. The director was Joe Donovan, a music teacher in the Boston Public Schools. Billy was a good drummer and became well known around town as someone who could really keep the beat. My mother said his teacher thought he was very good. In fact, back then, everyone thought Billy would be the one to go somewhere with his drumming. When he was in the sixth grade the drum and bugle corps was invited to play at the Woodrow Wilson Junior High School. Mr. Donovan introduced "Little Billy" who was giving a drum solo. Another boy from our neighborhood, Georgie Nowland, joined the drum and bugle corps and began to play the trumpet. Within a few years he was soloing with a local orchestra. Years later, as Danny Davis, he founded the successful Nashville Brass.

Jake listened to Billy practice and couldn't wait until he was old enough to join the drum and bugle corps, which he did as soon as he turned seven. He played with them until he went to Dorchester High School, at which point he joined the school's drum and bugle corps. But he only played with them his freshman year. After that he was too busy with sports, listening to and playing music in clubs.

My father loved music. He played the cymbals in the American Legion Newspapermen's Post band, and we would go see them march in parades. He had a nice tenor voice and sang every morning while he shaved, usually ballads like "Deep in your eyes there's a song of love and it's wonderful music to me." During Prohibition he and three of his fellow printers would get together in our living room Sunday afternoons to drink his home brew and sing barbershop harmony. I learned a lot of popular music from listening to my father and also from our upstairs neighbors who played the piano. They would invite me up to listen when they bought new sheet music and I would sing along. And I sometimes sang along with my mother who usually confined herself to singing hymns while she worked in the kitchen. Pa always had the radio on when he was home, so we were used to hearing music all the time.

I sang in the choir at St. Brendan's and later, when I was trying out for the high school glee club, the director was pleased to know this because he knew I'd been well trained. They taught me to read music, although by the time my sister Mary got to high school, they'd stopped teaching that. My voice was good enough to get me into the Singing Platoon when I was in the WAVES, and Mary has sung in her church choir for more than 30 years.

My Uncle Paul was a big jazz fan, and he used to visit us when he was on leave from the Army. He was my father's younger brother and he would tell these great stories about musicians and sit beside the radio to listen to jazz. We loved it when he came so we would sit there and listen to the radio with him. I don't know how much of a role that played in Billy and Jake's interest in music, but that was probably one of the first times any of us heard jazz.

Billy bought our first record player in 1941 shortly after he got his first job. He kept it in his room, and he and Jake would play records when they practiced their drumming.

3

The Swingingest Drummer Boy in the Band of the Oil Belt

Three months before North Korean forces invaded South Korea, Airman John E. Hanna packed up his drumsticks in his old kit bag and joined the military. He hadn't yet completed his post-graduate year at Dorchester High, but he decided to sign up before hostilities began. It was a good choice on his part, as his years in the Air Force helped form him into the drummer he became.

The Army Air Force Band was created in 1941 as there was still not a separate Air Force. Those magnificent men in their flying machines had been serving in the Aeronautical Division of the Army Signal Corps as far back as 1907, but unlike the British, the United States did not create a distinct air force until 1947, when it was finally broken off from the Army. The 761st Army Air Forces Band was established in 1943 in Florida, moved to New

Jersey in 1944, then overseas to England, Belgium, and Germany. In 1947 it became the Air Force Band and the following year moved to Sheppard Air Force Base. The band traveled far more than Jake did since he spent his entire Air Force career at Sheppard.

Sheppard was located in Wichita Falls, in north central Texas. It was a big, busy base, home to the 3750th Technical Training Wing, which ran aircraft maintenance programs. Wichita Falls was a wealthy town of about 100,000 people, with—thanks to the oil boom several decades earlier—more millionaires per capita than any other town in the United States. The band became known as the "Band of the Oil Belt." And the music fans on and off base kept the band busy.

The band's mission, as described in a report prepared the year after Jake arrived, was to help raise morale and to play for all required military ceremonies and functions. In addition to providing music for military formation and ceremonies, the band provided concert music, dance orchestras and individual musicians for recreation and entertainment at Air Force installations. If "it was within its capacities," the band "strove to assist in the promotion of Air Force objectives and to enhance the prestige of the United States and the United States Air Force."

The morale of the 761st Air Force Band squadron was "estimated to be extremely high," the report stated, with no "AWOL's, confinements, or restrictions."

These stories come from Jake's family, fellow band members from the Air Force, and from his own interviews.

I didn't leave Boston until 1950, for the service. That was the first time I was ever really out of town. I went in the service in March of 1950. I got out in '53.

Jake Hanna, Cadence interview

The Air Force really shaped me. It shaped me very nicely.

Jake Hanna, BBC Interview

We didn't make much of a big deal when Jake joined the Air Force. He just went off one day, and then there wasn't as much drumming coming from the front bedroom. I think my brother Billy was probably more aware of his absence than Eleanor and I.

Mary Hanna Howard

I could actually play a show better than most guys who could read [music], and when I went in the service in 1950 before the Korean War, it got me out of a lot of duty. I never did learn to read until I had a good job in an Air Force band. Lloyd Morales was great to me, got me faking my way through those Sousa marches.

Jake Hanna in Jazz Journal

When I went in the service I didn't know how to read [music]. But I learned real quick, in about two days — two days of wood-shedding, that's how I could get in the band. The guy who taught me was Sergeant Lloyd Morales, who turned out to be a friend. He learned how to play in the service and when he got out he could really play. (Later he played in Vegas with Lainie Kazan, Mitzi Gaynor, Les Brown, and Skinny Anderson). He's the one who got me in the band. He sort of hid me so they couldn't audition me. I could play shows by sight — I learned to play from the front of the acts I saw. All those acts showed up in the service at the USO. I remembered their acts so I could play; I didn't have to read the music. The only difference is I was playing from the rear, from the back of their act. They sent me out every Sunday to play when I was in basic training. They paid me 9 dollars, not bad for the service when you're only making 42 bucks a month.

Jake Hanna, BBC interview

I got married six months after Jake went into the Air Force, and he sent me $50 for a wedding present. That was very generous of him, because I doubt he earned much money. Later my sister Mary told me that she wrote to him and said he'd better send me a nice present.

Eleanor Hanna Judge

[Chip Deffaa] In the service ... Hanna drummed, both on the base (having to beat a bass drum at maximum strength for hours so troops could march to it was useful experience, he says) and also, as time permitted, off the base. Although he couldn't read music, he was able to play for the shows at a theater.

"I knew every act. How? I had seen every act that came through the RKO Theater in Boston six years earlier. I knew the trampoline act. I knew the guy with the newspaper act (he sat there and read a newspaper — you know, some funny licks). I knew the acts with the falling-away suit. I knew what to do."

Jake Hanna as told to Chip Deffaa

I met John in late 1951. (I'm probably one of the few people who called him John, and for some reason he always responded). I had just completed band school and was assigned to the 761st Air Force Band in Wichita Falls, Texas.

The day I got there someone stuck a string bass in my hand and said let's play and off we went. I remember wondering why the guy with the funny accent always seemed to be smiling at me, and one night when we played a job together I asked him. He said they hadn't had a bass player for a year so he was really happy to see me. That was the beginning of a lifelong friendship. When I got married he was one of the few people invited to our house for dinner.

One night a couple of the guys got very drunk and stole a motorcycle that they dragged upstairs to the second floor of the barracks. They got it started and were about to drive it around when someone said the AP — the Air Police — were coming. I never could figure out how they got it up in the first place or back down the stairs to hide it behind the barracks, but they managed.

The AP came upstairs, shone his flashlight around the exhaust-filled room and asked, "Did anyone see a motorcycle?"

John sat up in his bunk and in his thickest Boston accent said, "Yeah, man it went thattaway," pointing towards the fire escape.

The entire bay broke up, and we couldn't stop laughing for at least ten minutes. I think the AP threatened to take us all to the brig.

Over the years we spent together we played in many different groups, from small combos to large bands, and I particularly remember how we'd play time together. We'd start very slow, and then speed up until we were going as fast as we could for as long as we could. I would stick a piece of music in front of me and away we'd go and "Thou Shalt Not Rush or Drag" during his drum break or he would let you know in no uncertain terms.

Jack LaSpina

Jake called my mother one day to say he'd been mustered out and would be home in 4 or 5 days. He didn't actually show up for another year or so.

Mary Hanna Howard

Jimmy Dorsey Knew *Him*

Richard Boubelik

I joined the Air Force in Feb 1951 and was sent to Sheppard Air Force Base in Texas. The band guys all lived together in an old World War II-vintage wooden barracks, and we primarily did dance and entertainment stuff. The big band played at the USO where they had two shows on Sunday afternoons, but our main work was as a dance band for various NCO and Officers Clubs. Jack LaSpina, Jake, and I also formed a trio to play at the Officer's Clubs. We performed for marches and military purposes once a month or so, playing march songs, and then between numbers, the drummers would do rim shots on the snare and lots of tremendous drum cadences. Jake and the other drummers had a really good beat and sounded great, but the general and the other reviewers wanted the marches played straight instead of the swinging stuff that wasn't as good for marching.

We rehearsed every day, though we had lots of free time to play touch football. Compared to most guys in the service, our life was pretty plush. We complained, but in all honesty we knew we had it good. The drummers practiced all the time, though, working hard, hour after hour.

Jake was a terrific drummer even back then. He practiced seven or eight hours a day on those little rubber pads with an exercise book in front of him. There was never any question about what he wanted to do. We usually had about four drummers at any one time. One of them, a fellow from South Carolina, was well educated in band school and very interested in the technical aspects of drumming but could care less about jazz. He and Jake would sit down and practice together for hours, and Jake really appreciated him despite his lack of interest in jazz.

One of the things that first struck me about Jake was that he didn't drive. How could you be a drummer and not drive! That was almost unbelievable to me. You have to be able to lug your drums around. He didn't like to fly either. We played lots of gigs in nearby towns for public relations, but once we had an event in Amarillo and we had to fly there, and Jake was worried sick about flying.[9]

Because it was such a large base, the clubs were booming every night. There were a lot of career men who were older than us, and the NCO clubs had bands seven nights a week. Professional bands like Billy May and Jimmy Dorsey even came there to play. Amazingly, everyone seemed to know about Jake. The word had gotten around, and some of the professional musicians remembered him from previous visits. They knew how good he was, and they talked to him as though he were a peer, even though he was just 19 or 20. These were guys we heard on the radio, but *they* had heard of Jake. Everyone liked him, but it wasn't because he cozied up to them. He was always upbeat, on the level, never insulted anyone or tried to turn them off and was always happy ... unless someone was discussing—or playing—lame music.

The band group was a good bunch of guys with very different back-grounds and levels of education. We had some real characters. Whenever there was a storm, one fellow was so afraid of the thunder and lightning he would hide under his cot. Another fellow, a preacher's son, would sleep all the time, like Beetle Bailey in the comics. One guy got a hole in his shoe, and he took the little cards of sheet music that the trumpeters and trombonists and sax players clipped to their instruments, and he stuck in his shoe to plug the hole. We weren't military at all, and we didn't look like soldiers either. One Monday morning we were on parade, in our fatigues, maybe looking a little more unkempt than usual after the weekend. After we finished the Captain came over, looked us up and down, and said, "Fellas, I know you're a bunch of musicians, and we make allowances for that, but ... but ... but ... Goddamn it!" He had to say something.

But Jake still stood out. He and some of the guys used to go to the mov-ies, and when they got back, Jake would re-enact the entire movie for us. I

---

9   Jake wasn't actually scared of flying, but the low-flying DC-3s he traveled on in the Air Force made him airsick.

saw some of the movies later, and they were never as good as the way Jake re enacted them. He recited some of the scenes word for word, embellished it with expressions. Others doing the same thing might give you an impression or paraphrase, but not him.

Jake had a sharp mind and was focused on his music, but his intelligence shone through.

First Guy I Met in New York

Jake Hanna (From a 1993 Cadence Magazine interview)

First guy I ever met in New York City was Charlie Parker, 'cept for the bartender. First furlough in 2 years ... '52 ... the war was goin' on and on. The guy said, "You're gonna have to take a furlough, I know you been here on duty longer than the other guys, so this time you go for Thanksgiving." My friend and I, we drove all the way from Texas to New York City, we get out of the car, the other guy driving us up was from Boston, let us out, we been in this car for 3 days ...we're lookin' at the President Hotel, we're a little too far north, we're up on 54th Street, we walk down the street and we saw this thing up top that said Gene Krupa/Cozy Cole. I said, "There's a bar right underneath there, what say we go in there and get a bottle of beer or some-thin' to quench our thirst." Went into the bar, 3 o'clock in the afternoon ... there's a guy cuttin' lemons, and this joint was called "Le Downbeat," it was owned by the guy that owned Birdland, very small club ... a set of drums up there, a set of vibes. I says, "You have music in here?" He says, "Oh yeah, we have music in here." "Who plays?" "Well, we got a band that plays 7 nights a week, Chuck Wayne, Eddie Shaughnessy, Don Abney, Candido on the congas." I said, "Geez that's pretty good. Is that your main band?" He says, "No the main band is Max Roach, Percy Heath, John Lewis, Bill Harris, Kai Winding and Zoot Sims." "That's the main band?" "Yeah, but ... tonight is our off-night band. That same quartet plus we have Milt Jackson, that's what those vibes are for, we have Percy Heath, Kenny Clarke, John Lewis, Miles Davis and the leader's a guy named Charlie Parker." I went "gulp."

First time in New York, first time out of a car into a joint, and this is what I bump into. And as he's tellin' me this the door opens and a gust of snow comes in and one guy with a big bag with a turkey leg sticking out of the top

… Kai Winding comes in with a Homburg and a felt collar. And he says, "Put it down here, Charlie" … and Charlie puts the bag down, it's Charlie Parker. I said, "Geez, … can we buy those 2 guys a drink?" The guy says … "Two soldiers want to buy you guys a drink." Kai says, "I don't drink with strangers." Charlie says, "Well, I do." Kai says, "Well, I'll see you later." He left and Charlie Parker came down and talked with us for four hours. The nicest guy I ever met in my whole life.

CHAPTER

4

Mustered Out

Jake got out of the Air Force in September 1953 and went on the road with $400.28 of separation pay and "no wounds received as a result of enemy forces."[10] It took him more than a year to work his way back to Boston, where he moved back into his room at the family home and began playing wherever he could find a gig. He continued studying and took drum lessons from the great Stanley Spector.

Eventually he decided to use his GI Bill benefits to study music. So on January 16, 1956, he submitted his application to the Berklee School of Music. In the section that asked what date he proposed to enter, he wrote "1/16/56"—apparently he planned to start that afternoon. He enrolled for ten courses that semester and began bicycling the four and a half miles between Dorchester and Berklee's downtown Boston location at 284 Newbury Street[11].

---

10 According to his DD214, Report of Separation from the Armed Forces of the United States.

11 Charlie's Eating and Drinking Saloon is now located at 284 Newbury Street.

Berklee School of Music began life as Schillinger House, founded eleven years earlier by MIT graduate–pianist–composer-arranger Lawrence Berk to teach the Schillinger System of harmony and composition he had studied under its developer, Joseph Schillinger. Most music schools at the time focused primarily on classical music, but this new institution offered training in jazz and commercial music. Most of the early students were professional musicians, and soon World War II veterans began to attend under the G.I. Bill. Within a few years enrollment had grown from the initial 50 students to more than 500. By the time Jake enrolled the name had been changed to reflect the broader scope of instruction. Learning from practitioners was emphasized, and working musicians were hired as faculty members.

Outside of school there were plenty of places for the musician-students to play, and Jake kept busy. He got involved in the Jazz Workshop that Charlie Mariano, Herb Pomeroy, and Ray Santisi had set up a few years earlier. It was oriented toward the needs of working musicians who would learn by playing and working together. They got the best of the local players to teach there. Students would show up with an instrument and a dollar, half of which went to the teacher and half to the house. Storyville, George Wein's nightclub, was nearby in the Hotel Buckminster in Kenmore Square, and the musicians performing there would stop by too, so students might get a lesson from George Shearing or Louis Bellson. Jake later became the house drummer at Storyville. The Stable, a nightclub just outside Copley Square, showcased jazz seven nights a week, employed many of Charlie Mariano's friends — including Jake — and featured Herb Pomeroy's big band. And there was always Izzy Ort's, a dive next door to the RKO, where bands were booked practically round the clock.

Jake's Berklee classmate, Toshiko Akiyoshi, invited him to join her trio to play at the Hickory House that summer and the following three summers. He returned to school for the 1956 fall semester but his performing schedule got so busy that it began to conflict with his classroom studies. He was playing at Storyville when Marian McPartland came in one night and invited him to work with her. Subsequent gigs with Buddy Morrow, Al Vega, Harry James,

Maynard Ferguson, Duke Ellington and others took him on the road again and eventually moved him to New York.

Jake stayed in touch with Marian and Toshiko over the years. He worked with them occasionally, and in the 1970s, he was responsible for bringing both of them to record for Concord Jazz.

These stories come from Jake's Berklee classmates, current faculty and administrators, fellow musicians, and from his own interviews.

When I got out [of the Air Force] I was stranded in Texas.... Then Tommy Reed offered me a gig ... I only had four bucks to my name, so he sent me $9 for the bus fare to Shreveport, Louisiana to join the band. (Come to think of it, my salary wasn't much more than that bus fare.) I went with Tommy for two weeks but wound up staying for over a year. [I] left the band in Kansas City, returned to Boston, and started playing with local groups again and studying drums with Stanley Spector.

Jake Hanna, as told to Marian McPartland

I joined Tommy Reed's territory band, and I sat down in Kansas City for a while with him ... I'll tell you how you got the gigs in those days. Either you hung out in musicians' bars or you played jam sessions. (They don't have many jam sessions any more.) Well, Ted Weems' band had a jam session out in some joint, and one guy said, "Jeez, the drummer's leaving soon. Will you be interested in going with the band?" I said, "Yeah." I was making $100 a week. I went with Ted for $20 or $30, something like that — very low. Of course, hotels weren't very much either: $25 a week, $3 a day. But Ted had a very good band. He had one of the better books I played.

Jake Hanna, Cadence Magazine

[Stanley Spector] There is no other teacher for me. Many of them are so busy with the hands, building technique. Having "good hands" has nothing to do with playing jazz ... You've got to do first things first — learn to keep time and swing — the basic things a drummer is supposed to do, but you can't just do it right off the bat; it takes a while.

Jake Hanna, as told to Marian McPartland

I went to Berklee because that was the place. All the guys went there after the service. That's where the action was. Never have seen anything like it in the world. What an experience!

Like most of the other guys at Berklee then, I used the GI Bill to pay the way. The place was crawling with good players preparing to enter or re-enter the civilian job market. We were all playing catch up.

Jake Hanna, Downbeat Magazine

Berklee qualified to accept students on the GI Bill, and veterans were a big part of the early growth of the school. It was a very supportive place for musicians like Jake. Many of the GIs had played in the service bands and Berklee helped to strengthen them musically.

Lee E. Berk

There were only 140 people when I went there ... Toshiko, Charlie Mariano, Gene Cherico, Bill Chase, Bill Berry, Gordy Brisker, Bobby Freedman ...They all did very well for themselves.

Jake Hanna, Cadence Magazine

I met Jake in January 1956 when we both started at Berklee College of Music. We had some classes together, and he would make remarks in class that other people laughed at, but because I understood very little English I didn't know what he was saying.

Berklee was a small school back then, and lots of the students were on the GI Bill. I was on a scholarship, and there weren't many young kids the way it is today. Some of the students, like Jake, were already professional musicians.

Jake and I played together for quite some time, both in school and afterwards. We spent two months at a time at the Hickory House, a long time to play in one place. Other musicians would come in to hear us. *Time Magazine* took a picture of us in 1958.

There was a performer who played at a club and got all his material from Jake. Later on he played on one of the late night TV shows and did the same routines he got from Jake.[12]

Toshiko Akiyoshi

The Toshiko Trio, with Gene Cherico, had a lot of fun, some of the most enjoyable times of my life. Our first job was at London House in Chicago. Real great joint, Eddie Higgins had the intermission gig. Then the Modern Jazz Room in Cleveland. Then we played at the Hickory House in New York. We worked there every summer from '56-'60.

Jake Hanna BBC interview

I met Jake while I was at Berklee. We'd spend the whole day around there. Some afternoons we'd go to Laurel and Hardy or W.C. Fields movies. Jake was deep into W.C. Fields. We hung out quite a bit, went out to eat. We took ensemble classes with Herb Pomeroy, Ray Santisi, or Bob Share, and also ear training, theory, arranging. It was a healthy environment because there were so many talented people.

Paul Fontaine

I first met Jake while I was playing with Toshiko at Storyville. Jake was a student at Berklee at the time. Some mornings I'd see him at a coffee shop down the street from the club, and he'd be laying out his vitamins on the table.

---

12 Probably Charlie Callas, though not confirmed.

I heard him play, and I knew he would turn out to be one hell of drummer. He really impressed me with his brush work and was one of the wittiest persons I ever met.

Joe Porcaro

Jake was highly respected by all other musicians surrounding him because of his natural talent and for his ability to extend the same to them. His sense of perfect timing and dynamics always led others to follow, for they knew they could totally depend on his consistent rhythmic, swinging support. These two important elements were accepted then and now as benchmarks for the success of any and all solo/small band/big band performances at the Jazz Workshop and The Stables and other local venues. Jake delivered unselfishly.

Jake was able to engage his associates with a spontaneous, infectious sense of humor and was known to take pages from vaudevillians of the day, especially one reputed high-end imbiber named W.C. Fields.

Ray Santisi

Berklee College of Music was a great school, lots of great cats there. I first met Jake when he was playing in Herb Pomeroy's band, and I was in Peter Cutliffe's band. We had lots of rehearsals together so I hung out with the Pomeroy guys, and Jake and I got to be quite friendly. Even then he was a character, a funny guy, always a one-liner hanging out there.

Lennie DiMuzio

Jake and I met in Herb Pomeroy's B Band around 1956. I wasn't enrolled at Berklee at that time, because it didn't grant degrees. But I wanted to be there. Herb had a wonderful big band that played regularly at The Stables, across the street from Storyville. We all wanted to be in it, but the wannabees were in the B band. We must have been good, though, because Jake and I and about 10 other guys from the B Band all wound up in the '62-'65 Woody Herman Band.

Phil Wilson

Berklee was just about the only place for someone like Jake to study at that time, one of the few places outside a bandstand where you could find like-minded people. Although jazz is now established as one of the great musical traditions, people tended to look down on it back then. The few other places that taught it didn't even call it jazz because it had such a negative association; they called it "stage band." It was an unconventional path for a young musician to follow. So for Jake to meet Herb Pomeroy and other musicians like him who were crazy about this kind of music was a great source of affirmation. It was courageous for young people in 1956 to make jazz their life. Students today can learn from that historical context.

Jake was probably one of the first great drummers to come through Berklee and started the tradition of great drummers there. Alan Dawson became the Herb Pomeroy of drums and percussion. In part because of them and other early students, you can argue that no place has had the impact of Berklee on drummers. Jake would be considered one of the pioneers at Berklee, one of the people who came here a decade after the place started, and went out in the world, did great things and was a great representative of the school. He played with Toshiko, another pioneer. To affiliate with her on the original path she carved out for herself ranks him up there among the greats.

Roger Brown

I ... played money dates in a trio with Gene Cherico on bass and Toshiko on piano. (No one knew she had a last name then). Herb Pomeroy and Ray Santisi were students with me — later they went on the faculty. Bill Berry was also there. Unlike most of the other guys I didn't go much into the writing end. I was glad to be able to read. As I remember it, the week I left Berklee, Santisi was still daring me to find middle C. One of the guys I learned the most from was Pomeroy. Watching him run down a chart, guiding the players into their parts — putting it all together — was a real education.

Jake Hanna, Downbeat Magazine

When many veterans with limited formal music education were suddenly thrust into required courses — arranging for bands, harmonic theory, required piano lessons (even for drummers) — the classes seemed to take on a Dirty Dozen atmosphere. I was teaching a theory class that Jake and several veterans were taking. I was working my way around the class asking for definitions of terms related to harmony. The definitions were those found in the Schillinger, with its highly mathematical approach to harmony. Jake was asked to give the verbal definition of what was called a G6/4, a group of three chords with the one in the middle having the fifth in the bass. In his wonderfully spontaneous way, and with a somewhat whining W.C. Fields delivery, Jake said, "Ah yes, a G6/4. A group of three men walking down the street, the one in the middle having a fifth in his back pocket!"

Ray Santisi

I met Jake after he got out of the service and came back to Boston. I started the Al Vega Trio in 1950 at the Hi-Hat, and he played with me, but not regularly because he was busy and always going out on the road.

Jake always used to say to me, "The Al Vega Trio, no mysteries." He meant you always knew what we were playing.

Al Vega

[Storyville] That was absolutely the best band I ever played with. Lou Carter and Champ Jones and I were the rhythm section. The front line was Buck Clayton, Vic Dickenson, Pee Wee Russell and Bud Freeman. The vocalist was Jimmy Rushing, one of the all-time great jazz singers and a fantastic human being. We just opened and played the intermissions and everything always went perfectly. Can you imagine? That was just a house band. George Wein owned the club and occasionally played a little piano in the band. Everyone loved George.

Jake Hanna, as told to Marian McPartland

I first met Jake in the early '50s. Boston was a city of good drummers, including Roy Haynes, Buzzy Drootin and Marcus Foster. Jake was the young one coming up, who was as good as all of them. So I hired him as the house drummer at Storyville. When Toshiko came from Japan, we asked her to record for Storyville Records and we suggested she use Jake on drums. It was a beautiful session and it helped to get both Toshiko's and Jake's names known nationally.

Jake recorded a record with me and the Newport All-Stars in 1959 for Atlantic Records. It was one of the best records I ever made with Buck Clayton, Vic Dickenson, Pee-Wee Russell and Bud Freeman. It was a hall of fame group of musicians. Jake was a major contributor to that record.

Jake's style was that of the great swing drummers — Buddy Rich and Jo Jones. He could swing like mad and was equally adept at small combos and big bands. Not only was his playing great, but his sense of humor and the joy he brought to the job literally made people play at their best.

George Wein

[Buddy Morrow] That was a good job, I liked that job. A guy named Walt Stuart was writing some real good arrangements for him. There were a lot of good guys in that band. Dick Johnson was a star ... a real good player and a great guy. Jesus. You couldn't ask for a better human being than that guy.

Jake Hanna, Cadence Magazine

I left [Buddy] to go in the Hickory House with Toshiko and I worked every summer at the Hickory House, from '56, '57, '58 and '59. That was a very important thing for me because you could walk in there, have a drink and we sat in between the bar, you know, the oval bar you sat in between. So the guys would come in, Phil Woods would come in, hear me and says, yeah, I like this guy. Says, you wanna work your night off Monday over in Jersey? I said, sure, okay. I got to work with him and Chuck Wayne. And then Chuck got me a lot of stuff, and Nat Pierce and Gus Johnson come in, heard me, they hired me for something...I was off and running after that. I went to New York with a job, I didn't go down there looking for work. I was right on display for them to come out and hear every night if they wanted to hear it. Bobby Hackett finally comes in, he says, okay, come on over to Condon's and play. So I made a segue way from there till 1960 with Bobby, played at Condon's.

Jake Hanna, Cadence Magazine

I met Marian [McPartland] in Boston when I was playing behind Anita O'Day. She had a horrible piano player, and Marian came to sit in. Instantly it sounded right, it sounded very good. We fit in good.

She said "Boy, you sound terrific. How come it sounded so lousy before?"

I said, "Because you weren't here, that's why. When you came up you made it sound great."

She said, "I'd sure like to hire you on."

I said, "I need a job."

Jake Hanna, BBC interview

Jake was responsible for the tempo at which "And We Listened" was recorded.

I had mailed the music to Maynard some time before the band did the "Message From Newport" album. My tune got thrown in at the end of that session because they needed a few more minutes of music to fill out the side. Maynard kicked it off at a very fast tempo and they read the piece through for the first time. Now, before I sent the music to Maynard, Herb Pomeroy let me run it down with his band one night before the gig at the Stable to make sure the parts were copied accurately. Jake happened to be there. After the read-through with Maynard's band in the studio, Jake told him that the tune should be a bit slower. Time was running out at the session so they called for a take right away. Based on what Jake had told him, Maynard kicked it off, that second reading got recorded, and that's what ended up on the album.

Bob Freedman

Buddy Morrow and Maynard were truly great guys to work for. They always took responsibility for everybody else's mistakes. If someone hit a clam they would immediately say it was their fault.

Jake Hanna as told to John Tumpak

[Harry James was] in Boston and they were up at a record store, and Sammy Firmature (Harry's jazz tenor player) . . . spotted me. He says, ". . . I want you to meet Harry. We're up around the corner here." . . . I just left Maynard Ferguson. Anyway, I went in the store, and Harry was there with a couple of guys, and they're listening to that particular record "Message From Newport." He says, "How'd you like the drummer on that record? I liked that." He loved Maynard, he didn't mean I had some unbelievable chops. Says, "Well here's the guy right here, the drummer." He says, "You are? Well, come out and play with my band. Come out to Chicago to play with us."

Jake Hanna, Cadence Magazine

I had a chance to join Harry James — I auditioned with him too. He liked me right away, said, "You got the job. Send your drums out to the airport, and my wife will pick them up."

I went to Railway Express, the guy says, "Where they going?"

"To the airport in Las Vegas."

"To the Harry James Orchestra? Just send them to the airport?"

"Yeah," I said, "Harry's wife is gonna pick them up and take them to the club."

"OK." The guy took the drums, left, two seconds later I hear a rap on the door and the guy's back.

"Betty Grable is gonna pick up your drums!?"

"That's right."

"*Betty Grable* is gonna pick up your drums!? Who are you?" he said. "Who *are* you?"

"Nobody," I said. I'm just Harry's new drummer."

"Betty Grable is gonna pick up your drums!? Damn," he said, "I wish *I* played the drums."

He couldn't believe it. One of the most famous gals of all time, and one of the nicest too.

Betty Grable picked up the drums and brought them to the club in her station wagon.

Jake Hanna, BBC interview

She brought 'em to the wrong place . . . left 'em in the back room. I used Buddy Rich's stuff for a while. Louis Bellson happened to be in the other room. He spotted 'em, he said, "What are you doing playing Buddy's stuff? Your stuff has been back there for a week."

Jake Hanna, Cadence Magazine

When Jake was playing with Harry James, Harry used to go "one, two, one, two, three, four," with his back to the band, but his shoulders were slower than the tempo. So Jake finally asked him, "Harry, should I take the tempo from your shoulder, from the piano or just play it at the tempo we usually play it?" Harry said, "Jake you're the leader." Jake said, "Do you really mean that?" Harry said, "Yes."

Jake said, "Okay, you're fired."

Roy Burns

Jake told me that when he was playing in Las Vegas in the '60s, he was relaxing in the lobby of his hotel one morning when Count Basie walked through the lobby with his valet. He nodded at Jake as he passed, then paused at the entrance to the casino, stopped, turned, pointed at Jake, and said, "HANNA! You **SWING!**" Basie continued on into the casino, but his valet came back to Jake and said, "He doesn't tell that to just *everyone*, you know." With shaking hands Jake replied, "I know! See me *shaking*?"

Hal Smith

[A jam session in Columbus, Ohio, with Bobby Hackett and Dave McKenna led to Hackett inviting Hanna to play with him at Condon's in New York.]

"I said, 'You kidding? To get off the road again? Yeah.' In those days, you could get a place to stay in New York. I got a place for $80 a month, plus hot plate, on 48th Street, the Burnham ... from Bobby Hackett I went with Duke Ellington for 10 or 15 days until they could find Sam Woodyard again."

Jake Hanna as told to Chip Deffaa

A bunch of us lived in a building at 339 W. 48th Street starting around 1962. Drummer Lou Malin's mother owned the building, and he lived on the first floor next to Gene Williams. Jake took that apartment after Gene moved out. I lived on the second floor, Bill and Barbara Potts lived above me, and Herbie Powell lived above them. Joe Ciavardone lived in the basement; he was the super in between trombone gigs. Bobby Donavan lived on the third floor, and at various times Gene Cherico, Nick Travis and Barbra Streisand also lived there

Dick Sheridan

In New York, Jake and I were both very much on the scene at John Popkin's Hickory House, where he appeared many times with Marian McPartland, and we alternated sets.

Jake was always into some kind of mischief, creating jokes and generally enlivening the room from the raised oval bandstand in the middle of the great Jazz Club-Steakhouse with humongous murals of great prizefighters painted on the walls, and glass-walled storage areas with carcasses of cows hanging inside, from which chefs gleaned their succulent treasures.

His playing was a great compliment to Marian's Trio ... there was an immediate joy and lightness. You could hear Marian and the bassist clearly at all times. He knew the lessons of Papa Jo Jones: "If you can't hear the pianist, you're too loud."

Suezenne Fordham

... I used to have supper with him [Coltrane] every night at Horn & Hardart's at 54th Street and Broadway. I knew who he was, and he used to see me around but we never even said a word, we just ... sat at a table every night like supper partners....like in your house you never talk to your father or your mother, supper's just eaten...that's how we were. And I'd go around to hear him, and he'd come around the corner, hear us with Toshiko, but we never even said hello. Sort of a shy guy, a very, very nice man.

Jake Hanna, Cadence Magazine

Mary Hanna invited me to her family's apartment. We came in unannounced and Jake was walking around in his underwear. I was embarrassed, but Mary just said she had a friend with her and he ran into another room and soon reappeared fully dressed, charming and unconcerned. We later saw him play at George Wein's Storyville in the Buckminster Hotel. I *loved* the jazz scene and knew that Jake was a great drummer, so we went there several times to hear him play. Mary likes to say that I was his first fan, but I like to think that I had a crush on him.

I went to New York with another group of Dorchester girls a few years after that, and insisted we go to a club in Greenwich Village to hear Jake play with Marian McPartland. We found the place and naively asked the waiter when the music would start. To our dismay, we were told not until 10 or 11 that night. We girls couldn't afford to sit there buying expensive Cokes all night, so we had to leave. I was so disappointed because I really wanted my friends to hear him play with the great Marian McPartland.

I watched him later on "The Merv Griffin Show" and kept track of his career. My love of jazz is still strong, and I date it back to when I first met Jake and heard him play.

Joanne McDermott

C H A P T E R

5

Thundering and Swingin'

Jake first heard "The Herd" sometime in 1945 or '46 at the RKO Theatre in Boston. He went there expecting to hear his idol, Dave Tough, and when the lights went up, he was disappointed at first to see a light-haired man on the drums. After Don Lamond played, though, Jake had found himself a new idol. And about 12 years later he found himself on the band.

Woody Herman, a clarinetist and saxophone player who became one of the most popular big band leaders of the 1930s and '40s, had a series of bands that were collectively referred to as "The Herds." They played almost continuously from 1936 to 1986, and employed some of the best musicians of that time. He began his career as a bandleader with "The Band That Plays the Blues" in 1936, which someone renamed Woody Herman's Herd in the 1940s. He formed his Second Herd in 1947 and the Third Herd in the early 1950s. Although subsequent Herds didn't necessarily have names, the '62-'64 band was generally known as the Young Swinging Herd.

Woody's bands were always characterized by their rhythmic drive and intensity and by the enthusiasm of the players. In Herman's autobiography, jazz critic Gene Lees is quoted as saying that "Woody had an astonishing capacity to spot talent before it was particularly obvious to anybody else ... the list of careers that he either made or advanced is staggering."

Jake played with Woody for several months in late 1957 to '58, and then from 1962 to '64, in what many agree was the greatest swinging band.

The personality of the band was often built around the drummer, and Woody had some of the best. Over the course of 50 years, they included Dave Tough, Don Lamond, Buddy Rich, Jake, Jeff Hamilton, Shelley Manne, Ed Soph, Joe LaBarbera, Jim Rupp, Chuck Flores, John Von Ohlen and Shadow Wilson.

These stories come from Woody Herman musicians who played with Jake, and from his own interviews.

When I first came on the band in '57, we needed drummers. I kept pushing for Jake even though I was a newcomer on the band. "Oh, man, Woody, you should get Jake Hanna, he's a great drummer." After six months or so I finally had convinced someone that he was good. We were playing someplace near Boston and because of a misunderstanding with Abe Turchen, I got fired in the middle of the job. There were two sets of stairs, one on each end of the bandstand. As Jake was coming up to sit in with the band, I was going down the other side. So I got him on the band, but I never got to play with him on the band until years later.

Bill Berry, "Chronicles of the Herd"

When I auditioned with him, Woody wouldn't let me read the drum book, wouldn't let me read out the trumpet part or any part. He just wanted to see how I felt. But every chart he pulled out I knew by heart because I had the records of them, "Four Brothers," "Apple Honey," "Woodchopper's Ball," "Good Earth." He pulled up all swinging tunes. He didn't care what the ballad was. He said okay, play this one. I ate it up.

Jake Hanna, BBC interview

CADENCE: When you came into the Woody Herman band, who did you replace?

Jake Hanna: First time I replaced Karl Kiffe, '57. This guy gave me the job with his condolences. (laughs) It was a lousy band, it was lousy.

CAD: Woody Herman spoke highly of you.

J.H.: Well, we were good pals.

CAD: What do you think you did for that band; what effect do you think you had on that band?

J.H.: Well, it just wasn't me...it was a combination of guys.

CAD: You were with him till about '57, right?

J.H.: Oh '57, that was a lousy one, nothing I could do about that, nothing. Nothing anybody could do with it. Fortunately we had Bill Harris. That was the highlight, but it wasn't enough to keep it afloat, you know. In the end they got Pete Jolly to play piano and Buddy Clark, and that helped.

CAD: Well, why was it a lousy band?

J.H.: Lead guys. Nobody could play together ... the pitch was all off, the time was different every bar and the pitch was up and down, slop and flop, Joe Romano didn't know what the hell to do then. Finally got Arno Marsh in there, that helped, but he wasn't playing the lead and Bill Harris didn't play much lead. And the other guys... just not a good band.

CAD: What do you think joining Herman did for you?

J.H.: Well, it got me working again. If you work a job...if a job's too bad you can't afford to stay there, let's face it.

Jake Hanna, Cadence Magazine

Jake was with the Herd briefly, only to return in 1962, becoming the drummer most associated with the "Swingin' Herd" of the early '60s.

Chronicles of the Herds

It was January 1962 and I had just finished a short stint with Harry James. Gus Johnson left Woody to stay in New York and I was hired to replace him in a sextet that was supposed to go out on the road. But before the road trip we were booked to play the Metropole in Manhattan with a big band Woody put together just for that engagement. That was a powerful band. Shelley Manne came in on our third night and we were really roaring. He called everyone in town and by the second set you couldn't get in and by the end of the evening we were booked all across the country:

That ended Woody's plans for the sextet. Gene Williams, the bartender, spread the word and every night the place was packed with musicians. Bob Haggart and Zoot Sims showed up a lot as did Joe Cronin, Woody's buddy from the Red Sox. Nat Pierce rewrote the book. We played the history of the Herman band, the `40s hits, the Four Brothers Band, and the Third Herd. As time went on we started playing our own arrangements of other songs like "The Days of Wine and Roses." Hank Mancini told Woody that it was the best arrangement of the song he ever heard. What a band and what a bandleader.

Jake Hanna as told to John Tumpak

'62 was one of the better bands to play with for the simple reason that Woody tried to incorporate into it the best of his previous bands. We had some new stuff come in by Nat Pierce and Bill Chase. Then we had the old stuff by Neal Hefti. We went all the way back to the '30s ... "Woodchopper's Ball." Then stuff from 1945, some of the best stuff ever written. "The Good Earth," "Sidewalks of Cuba." And we went up to the 1947-'49 band with the Four Brothers. Woody put it together as strictly a Four Brothers sound, eliminated the alto and had everything rewritten by Nat for three tenors and a baritone.

Jake Hanna, Chronicles of The Herds

"Jake is, I think, one of the most underrated drummers of all time," [Nat] Pierce told this writer.

Hanna had worked with innumerable jazz groups, large and small. He'd grown up during the bop era but his instinctive feel for a big band and how to drive it harked back to the great swing-era drummers.

Steve Voce, "Woody Herman Live in '64" liner notes

The Herd was booked into the Metropole in New York January 1–18. The band was forced to perform standing up because the 'bandstand' was little more than a shelf running the length of the wall behind the bar. The orchestra would perform, strung out in a single line abreast, with the brass lined up on Woody's left and saxes and rhythm to his right. It was next to impossible for the different sections to hear one another. Nevertheless, the band produced superb music. It is said that during its many engagements at the Metropole, the orchestra picked up the habit of playing standing.

Chronicles of the Herds

We were all up behind the bar at the Metropole, single-file ... There was a mirror. I could almost see them. But they were sort of in the dark down there. And only one mike. Single file. Lined up like this, sideways. We thought it was going to be a disaster. We said, "It'll never work; we can't go in there with new arrangements, we have to rehearse everything on the road." Woody says, "The sound will bounce right off the mirror instantly. I know it'll work." He was 100% right. I said, "No, it's going to go blip-blip-blip-blip-blip," but it didn't. It played like that.

There might have been a delay for the sound down the other end from the drums, but Bill Chase always looked in the mirror and he watched the hi-hats going up and down like that, and that's how he got his time. He'd have to wait one beat to get the start.... We always played that fast. One tune a set we played that fast. He'd just watch in the mirror like that. I was way down here and he down, down there. I'd look at him and he'd look—pow and we'd hit.

Benny Goodman came in and he says, "How the hell do you do this, Woody?" And Woody says, "It's all done with mirrors."

Jake Hanna, Cadence Magazine

In the early sixties I used to go hear Jake play with Woody, and then we'd go across the street to a bar called the Copper Rail where you could get a shot of booze or a beer for only thirty-five cents. We wove a dangerous path across Seventh Avenue. It was a great time for jazz in New York.

Johnny Varro

I wanted to be on the Woody Herman Band so I did my homework and found out what all the great drummers on the band had played. All of us who wanted to be on Woody's band used Jake's 1963 version of "Caldonia," which was faster than anything we'd heard before. We knew that if we could play it at the tempo that Jake played it for as long as it lasted, then we were ready to go on Woody's band.

Jeff Hamilton

And we went down to this bar, and they're serving this beer they make there ... this guy's happy to see 16 people roll in .... Well, we got so drunk ... And we get on the bus ... it's about 1 in the morning ... it takes about 6 hours to get to Chicago.

... we start driving ... the bus is rockin' ... everybody's drunk as a bat. Finally ... we had to answer the call to nature ... when we stopped ... we're out in the middle of nowhere ... with the headlights ... pointed right at this ... farmhouse.

"Where [do] we go?" "Go on the side of the bus." "We can't see." "Well go up against that wall I've got the headlights on."

16 guys get out and piss all over this guy's house ... and they're all growlin', sort of like a bunch of rock 'n' roll morons and then you see the window opening.

"Who's down there, what's goin' on?"

You hear, "Go back to bed you bum, we're still busy."

"Who is it dear?" He says, "I don't know honey, but there's 16 guys pissing all over our house."

They're scared to death, "Should we call the police?" "Oh I don't dare, a bus just pulled up and everybody just started pissin' all over our house."

I could hear them talkin', and we're down there really laughin' … it took us an hour to empty our bladders. We jump on the bus and off we go, but I can see this guy, the cop comin' up, he says, "What happened?" "Dunno officer, I was sound asleep and this bus pulls up and everybody gets out and starts pissing all over our house."

… Nat Pierce said, "Your house is on fire, we're takin' care of it, go back to sleep … Haven't you ever had a fire before? We're doing you a favor."

Jake Hanna, Cadence Magazine

I don't remember Jake driving. I'm not sure he even had a license when we were with Woody Herman in `62-`64. When we were on the road, we had a bus driver who was very bad, and always tired. He couldn't drive more than 25 miles out of town without pulling over and falling asleep. Nat Pierce always used to give people names. He called this guy "The Bus."

One morning we were down south, it was early, the sun had just come up, and the bus was moving so slowly that I couldn't imagine what was going on. So I woke up everyone and we went up front. There was Jake driving the bus while "The Bus" was sleeping in Jake's seat.

Paul Fontaine

Jake actually learned to drive in Florida when he was with Marian. They had to do a lot of driving and finally he took lessons so he could take his turn behind the wheel.

Denisa Hanna

When Woody Herman played at Lennie's on the Turnpike, it was the first time we had such a big band name play there. What an exciting night. I remember Jake, with his wiffle haircut, really bootin' the hell out of that band.

He came back again and did a Gretsch Drum Night for us. I liked to come up with good titles for the shows so I called this one "Drums Along the Turnpike."

Lennie Sogoloff

When he played at the Metropole in New York with Woody Herman's Herd, Jake told me his equipment at the time included a small Slingerland bass drum — the desired size of most modern drummers of the '50s and '60s. Playing opposite the Herman Herd was a trio with New Orleans drum pioneer Zutty Singleton. In contrast to the modernists, Singleton used larger bass drums; 26 to 28 inches in diameter. One night, as Jake went onstage with Herman, Singleton pointed to Jake's small bass drum and shook his head in disapproval. He then pointed to his own huge bass and made a nod of approval. As Jake walked past, he commented, "Yeah, Zutty. But I've got a big BAND!"

Hal Smith

In the early 1960s, when he was the chief propulsive force in the Woody Herman band, Jake used to do a routine, narrated by Woody, that might have been titled Drummer's Progress. It was a description of a boy drummer's development from the earliest stage, when he is unable to co-ordinate his hands and feet, through the phases of a career that takes him into such improbably disparate groups as Liberace's and Stan Kenton's. It was hilarious. But it was also a revealing demonstration of versatility, for Jake showed how one could and should play for different people, even if he did it as parody.

Gene Lees "Portraits in Jazz"

A guy by the name of Jack Ackerman, a tap dancer with the band, put that [humorous skit] together for us. It was the night that Sal Nistico joined the band in Dallas. It was an afternoon job at Lou Ann's.

Woody was out in front arguing with some lady customer, and I had to play a drum solo and I was playing real quiet. I was playing the brushes, and I got down real quiet and the customers were so dumb they didn't get it [the near-silence].... So I got indignant, and I started "swishing" the brushes and the people started laughing, the band started laughing and Woody and Jack Ackerman started watching it. Then I started playing like an "oaf," and then I started playing serious again and we took it out.

And Woody said, "We've got to find a way to use that!" We tried it a couple of times and got a few laughs. So Jack said, "Look, as long as you're going to do that, let me put it together for you." He's worked Bob Hope and Bing Crosby, and he knows how these things work. "Man," he says, "You start out like a dummy, take the dumb part as a high school drummer." Then he had me do a "Liberace." Woody would be announcing all this, and every now and then, he'd throw in something new to break the band up, because if the band wasn't laughing, the people weren't laughing.

Jake Hanna, Chronicles of The Herds

Jake loved Moxie.[13] Anytime we were someplace that sold it, he bought a case of it and stashed it under the bus.

Phil Wilson

Woody Herman is my favorite of all the bandleaders. I worked with a lot of guys—he's the best, as far as I'm concerned.

He's never sold out at all. Woody loves that excitement—it's probably why he's still sane. He's got a great sense of humor ... you have to. Oh boy, he's really paid some dues; I couldn't begin to

---

13   Moxie was of the first mass-produced soft drinks in the United States; its flavor was not as sweet as most soft drinks. In fact, it was quite bitter. Jake and Nat Pierce drank it with vodka.

tell you the headaches that guy's had. I couldn't do it—even if I had to. I wouldn't, either. He's a strong guy, still out there on that road. So is Basie, and so was Duke.

So when these young guys say they can't take the road—forget it; they're sissies. Woody's over 60 now, Basie's 70, Duke was 75.

Jake Hanna, interviewed by Les Tompkins (1975)

I first met Jake when I was about 4 or 5. He was one of my grandfather's favorite musicians and favorite people and Jake felt the same way about Woody. Denisa was good friends with my Mom so I saw them both when I was in LA. I loved him a lot and tried to stay in touch. He was a friend of the family.

He'd tell me "inside jazz" things and that was fun. He told me this story — it's in the Herds book, too — about how in 1967 my grandfather called him to ask if he'd come to play at the Detroit Auto Show. Afterwards they were heading out to the bar when they passed the room where Bobby Vinton was playing, and Woody said he wanted to catch his act. So they watched Bobby play the clarinet, and then the trombone, the sax, the bass, then the drums, then he played the piano, then he tap danced. He finally got through, and Woody looked over at Jake and said "That kid can't do *anything*!"

Tom Littlefield

I was on Woody's band in 1967. Jake came out to sub for about 3 weeks. He didn't want to have to set up and tear down the drums so he asked if anyone in the band would do that for him for $25 a week (it was 1967, remember). I said I would, so he showed how to set them up and repack them. He had one of those compact sets where one small drum fit inside a slightly larger one, and then those two went inside another one, etc. When he moved out to L.A and we started to run into each other, I reminded him of this. After that, when we worked together he would say, "Hey, you want to set up my drums?!"

Roger Neumann

I played with Woody for a week in Vegas sometime in the `70s to fill in between drummers. The guys in the band were still talking about Jake, how much they liked his playing and his great humor.

Frank DeVito

One of Jake's successors with Woody, my friend John Von Ohlen, told me that he had to take some time off from the band to have hemorrhoid surgery and that Jake bailed him out and filled in for him, circa 1967–68. So when I interviewed Jake for the Chase book, I mentioned in passing that I was aware that he played with Woody again a few years after departing in 1964.

Quoth Jake: "Oh yeah, that was for Johnny Boy. Poor guy — had to have a tochas operation."

Johnny Boy!! Jake was the first and only person ever to refer to John that way. And "tochas operation!" Never heard anyone refer to that medical procedure in those terms.

Jim Szantor

I worked with Woody a lot over the years. I was with him at his 40th Anniversary Carnegie Hall concert and put together a great little combo for him that played the Rainbow Room for a month in early 1984. That was the first time Scott Hamilton and Warren Vaché worked with Woody. Polly Podewell was the vocalist. I loved Woody and we had a great relationship. My wife Denisa and I went out with him a lot socially to have dinner and to go to clubs to hear bands play. He was quite a guy.

Jake Hanna as told to John Tumpak

Jake was the best drummer I ever worked with, and I've worked with some wonderful drummers. He was very sensitive behind a singer. He didn't just bang away, but used the brushes like nobody else. I knew he didn't want to work with lots of singers so I was honored that he would work with me.

I met him when we worked Woody's Rainbow Room gig together in 1984. We really hit it off and had a great time. Lots of people came in to hear us. Buddy Rich came in one night and remarked how much he liked Jake's playing. He didn't say nice things about a lot of people, but he loved Jake and admired his drumming.

I adored Jake. He was so easy to love. Everybody loved him.

Polly Podewell

A Magical Moment in Chicago

Jim Keltner

I never knew Jake in the early years. It was in Chicago, on my first trip away from home that I discovered him. I left Pasadena in 1962 to play a gig in Chicago. I wasn't making any money on the gig, so I couldn't afford to go out to a club. But someone said Woody Herman's band was playing at a club on Rush Street and Jake Hanna was playing the drums. I didn't know who he was, but they said you gotta see him; he's going to be sitting by the window, so you can hang out on the sidewalk and check him out. I thought that was cool, so I went down and stood out there on the sidewalk with a zillion other people and I was completely knocked out.

It was one of those magical moments that change your life. I've had quite a few: the time I heard Elvin Jones play with Coltrane in L.A. for the first time together; when I saw Philly Joe with Miles; when I saw Shelley Manne and his Men for the first time; Sonny Payne with Count Basie; or Billy Higgins in Pasadena practicing by himself at the Dragonwyck when it was just being built. Those are the moments that change your whole musical life. Then Jake Hanna. I was very young and I was just amazed by the fluidity in Jake's playing. He played so fast but powerful enough to kick the band. It was pretty, the technique was really sweet. It was the full package. I remember thinking *I have got to hear this guy play some more*. He really captivated my imagination on the drums.

I became a lifelong fan of Jake based on that gig. I didn't see him play again with big bands and large groups, just with small groups. And every time I'd see him I'd be amazed at how this was the same guy who was so dynamic and so powerful playing with that big band back in the early '60s, but now he plays really subtle and beautiful and soft. I think it was Jake and the way he played that helped me understand that I wanted to be able to play as quietly as he could and still generate a great feel like he did. That's the way he influenced me most. He showed me how to do that, showed me that was possible. I will always thank him for that.

I used to thank him all the time, but he never did take a compliment, he'd always make a joke. I think I got a little bit of that from him, too. Jake was an unusually beautiful, articulate player, and articulate in the way he lived. I loved the way he did interviews. He really spoke his mind. You could find the truth in there if you weren't afraid of it. He spoke from the hip.

I think I first met him at the Professional Drum Shop. That's where I usually met the guys from his era. I didn't get to hang out with him much. He traveled a lot so I missed a lot of his gigs, but I always knew he was there. I loved hearing people tell me they'd seen him and that he was fantastic. I knew what they meant.

The night Charlie Watts and I had dinner at Jake's with him and his wife Denisa was fantastic. Because Charlie is such a great fan of the era that spawned Jake, we watched some video, and Jake answered lots of questions Charlie had about how he felt about jazz. It was fun to get Jake talking like that and he told a lot of great stories. Later he gave Charlie a cymbal, one of his Chinas. It's the centerpiece of his collection.

They don't make 'em like that anymore. Jake was in that category.

CHAPTER
6

And Now Here's the Dear Boy Himself . . .

In 1965 Merv Griffin, a former radio and big band singer who had also performed on Broadway and in films, was launching a new talk show. His earlier show had run for several months in 1962–63 before being cancelled. The new show would be syndicated for the Group W division of Westinghouse Broadcasting in the hope that Merv could become a late-night TV rival to Johnny Carson. The show aired in multiple time slots throughout North America; some stations ran it in the daytime, some broadcast it opposite Johnny Carson's "The Tonight Show," and it was carried for many years in prime time on WNEW in New York. Merv's announcer-sidekick was the veteran British character actor Arthur Treacher, who had been his mentor. Treacher would introduce Griffin with the phrase: ". . . and now, here's the dear boy himself, Meeeer-vin!" after reading off the list of guests for that evening's show.

The show had an orchestra — studio orchestras existed only in television studios or recording or movie studios and did not perform public concerts or for audiences outside the studio—made up of skilled musicians, many of them delighted to get off the road, play a steady gig, and count on a regular weekly paycheck. That was enough for a while. But they didn't anticipate how little their own musical talents would be used and eventually it became frustrating for them. That's when Jake went into action and developed some of his more comic routines and quick one-liners, to the amusement of both his band members and the audience.

The band rehearsed about 4:30 in the afternoon, took a break, then the show taped at 7:30 in the Little Theatre on 44th Street between Broadway and 8th Avenue, next door to Sardi's.

In 1970 the show moved to Los Angeles and found a new home at CBS. Although Jake knew he'd miss New York and all his cronies, he decided to relocate. Not all the band members made the move, so new musicians were added in L.A.

Jake stayed at a hotel across from CBS, then with friends, then found permanent residence in Mid-City with A.J. Kahn, a jazz fan and cousin of drummer Tiny Kahn. He continued to record and take outside gigs whenever possible and kept things humming on the sound stage.

These stories come from musicians who worked with Jake on Merv's show, other musicians who knew him at the time, and from his own interviews.

I did about four different TV shows with Merv. Then in 1965 I had a chance to go to Europe for the first time to do some clinics. It turned out Merv's new show was starting at the same time, and I couldn't get a sub to cover the clinics, so Jake took my place on the show.

Roy Burns

I was doing nothing in New York, and one night [trumpeters] Bill Berry and Danny Stiles were at the other end of the bar at Jim and Andy's. Danny came over and asked me "Jake, do you read?" I said "Nope." He goes back and tells Bill I don't read. Bill says, "Ask him if he *can* read." He comes back and asks me. "Only if absolutely necessary," I tell him. He says, "Do you want a job? We're starting a new show."

"I'll do it." I told him, "But I gotta have the option of getting out of there any time I need to with no notice." He said okay. I went down to the first rehearsal, they brought in a new bandleader and he was an asshole, so I quit the first day and went to Chicago with Gene Krupa.

Jake Hanna as told to Rory Judge

Well, he was a very good guy to work for, Merv Griffin, very generous guy. And the main thing is, it was just a very good band.

Cadence: How much playing can you do … in that band?

None, you just play when the commercials are on, you play a little bit.

Jake Hanna, Cadence Magazine

A guest singer on the show agreed to an impromptu performance, and said to Jake, "Give me four bars." Jake called out the names of four of the New York City bars where musicians hung out: "Charlie's, Junior's, Joe Harbor's and Jim and Andy's!"

Bill Crow

Mel Brooks and Carl Reiner were guests one day, and people were panicking because Carl was late. When he got there he was berated by Mel. Carl explained that he had just been to the doctor and was told he had arrhythmia, to which Jake promptly responded "who could ask for anything more."

John LaBarbera

Kate Smith came on the show to sing "God Bless America." She had a new arrangement and instead of leading with a two-drum-beat Da Da Da Da before the final "God Bless America, my home sweet home," there was now a much longer set of triplets

Da Da Da Da Da Da Da Da Da and she was coming in early during the rehearsal, she just couldn't get it. She kept apologizing to the musicians, saying, "I'm sorry, I haven't done it like this before, and I don't know why I can't get it."

Well the triplets were the same as the ones on 'Caldonia' so finally Jake said to her, "Come in right after "what make you big hit so hard.[14]"

She laughed and said, "Thank you, I'll never forget it now."

Jack Benny was a guest, and Merv asked what he'd done that day. "I walked around town and went back to the old Edison Hotel where I lived in the `30s, with George Burns and Jimmy Stewart." Merv said, "Oh, our drummer lives there now." Jake stands up and Benny says to him, "I bet things have changed a lot since then," and Jake says, "Everything's changed except the sheets, Mr. Benny." It broke Jack up. It was an old line, but Jake's timing was perfect.

Another time Merv had a comedian on, and the first thing this guy would do was a pratfall, he'd somersault and land on his back. Nobody liked the guy. He came over to Jake and said, "When I fall, do a paradiddle and ratamacue and a boomp on the bass drum. Now let me hear it." Jake plays it. The guy says, "OK, do it again," and Jake did it again. "OK, he says, now let's try it from the top," and he comes out from behind the curtain and Jake goes "ting" on the cymbal. "No, no, no," the guy says. "That's where I want the boom crash." Jake says "OK, now I get it." The guy comes out again, Jake does something completely different. The band is trying to keep from cracking up. They did it a third time, and it just drove the guy crazy. He was so injured he couldn't open his act that way.

Jake was always coming up with funny names for the musicians. He called Ray Brown "Sun Ray," and "Sugar Ray," Cal Collins was "Taj MaCal" and Bud Shank was "Ravi Shank."

Michael Moore

---

14 The line in Caldonia was "what make your big head so hard."

Jake and the guys in the band could be pretty brutal to people — the ones without talent, of course — but Merv seemed to relish it.

Denisa Hanna

One afternoon during the show Merv set up a joke with the band. He announced that the drummer's wife had just had a baby, and the audience applauded. Then he said, "Will the happy father please stand up," and all the guys in the band got up. Later that day my mother got a call from one of her elderly relatives in Fitchburg (Mass) who said, "We didn't even know Jake got married."

Mary Hanna Howard

Jake was always a fun guy. He could make a joke out of anything. I remember when his brother came to New York to see the show. He was a character too.

Dick Hafer

I knew Gene Krupa, and I introduced my brother to him. Billy came down to see "The Merv Griffin Show," and afterwards we're walking past the Metropole and there's a big sign that said "Gene Krupa." I knew my brother idolized him since the `30s, so I said, "Let's go in and see him."

"See him?" he asked.

I said "Hey Chief, I'm a good pal of this guy, I never told you that." He says "Oh, bullshit."

So we see Gerry at the door and I say, "Hey, Gerry, this is my brother Billy," and he says, "Go up, Gene will want to see you." So we go up and there's Gene with his feet up and a towel around his neck and he's drinking a Tom Collins and watching the baseball game. He says, "Hey, come in," and I introduce him to Billy. They talked for 45 minutes while I watched the White Sox game. They kept talking back and forth. My brother really knew all those old bands, and they start talking about them, guys from the old neighborhood like Georgie Nowland, now he's Danny Davis and the Nashville Brass.

Jake Hanna as told to Rory Judge

I can still see Jake standing by the jukebox at Charlie's Tavern doing his W.C. Fields imitation.

Some Sundays around 5 a.m. when we left the bar, someone would start to feel religious and say, "Let's go to Mass" — it was the booze talking — so we'd head over to West 49th St. to St. Malachy's for 5 a.m. Mass. The priest would ask for someone to serve as an altar boy, and there were always volunteers, but some of these guys couldn't even walk up to the altar never mind serve. He would look us over — we were a motley crew of musicians, bartenders and waiters — and try to figure out if there was someone who could actually make it through the whole Mass without falling over or falling asleep. The one guy who made it through the entire Mass was Jake because he didn't imbibe the way the rest of us did and was always in good altar boy shape. I hadn't known he was Catholic, but I saw him at Mass one day, and he had his missal.

Dick Sheridan

Labor Day '70 I went out (to the West Coast) with Merv. We had a real good band in LA. We had Ray Brown and Herbie Ellis, Plas Johnson, Kai Winding.

We played ... bad music with good guys, 'stead of good music with bad guys. But if you get those guys like Sonny and Cher, those pop acts out there, they don't know the difference; they want it like their bad record. We had some lousy acts, God they were awful; those pop acts are so bad. It's all a waste of time with these musicians playing this junk. Rock 'n 'Roll, you know, there's nothing there, nothing to get your teeth into. Nothing you can do with the songs, nothing you can do with the music. It's too bad.

Jake Hanna, Cadence Magazine

All the musicians used to refer to Jake as the Mayor of Boston. He had that big Boston accent and told such great stories.

He used to call me Mundelow.

Mundell Lowe

Jake used to visit me in Vegas after Merv moved the show to LA, and one time I had a gig. He came to hear me play, then we went out to eat, then we went to the union hall and Jake drank two drinks to every one of mine, and we didn't get home until 5 am. He asked me for 6 Excedrin and to set the alarm for 7. Why? Because they were doing the show live that afternoon and he had a rehearsal at 10. I couldn't do that on so little sleep after a night of drinking.

Joe Locatelli

I was about 15 when Jake first came into the Pro Drum Shop in Los Angeles. He and Bob Yeager were great friends from way back, and I think he was staying at our house after he moved out from New York. He had a red car and I drove home with him to Northridge where Mom was making cioppino for dinner. Back then he used to come into the shop almost every day to hang out.

In the mid 70's he had me cut his bass drum in half and put hinges in it, and then he'd put the other drums inside so he could carry it around more easily.

He was a good close friend all the way to the end.

Stan Keyawa

My brother A.J. was a big fan of Jake's. When Jake was in L.A. he would crash at A.J.'s, as many musicians did, and they became great friends. After Merv Griffin moved the show out there, A.J. invited Jake to share the house and bought a Japanese piano so they could have jam sessions when everyone stopped by. On Saturdays my brother would cook a big pork roast and make cornbread and set up three televisions and all the guys would come over and watch three different football games. Jack Sheldon even wrote a song about AJ. called "Get Deep with Dr. Deep."

When A.J. got sick and time was running out he gave Jake the papers for the house and said he just had to pay what A.J. had originally paid, even though it had appreciated.

Jake invited me to the Jazz Festival in Sacramento the year A.J. died. I was very touched to see that they made an honorary mention of my brother which I really appreciated.

I really loved Jake. He was like family.

Jerry Kahn

You'd go nuts if you didn't get out and let off some steam. It's no use professional musicians of the caliber of Ray [Brown] and those guys sitting there [without much music to play]. You gotta get out there and play, man.

Jake Hanna as told to Les Tompkins

Shirley Bassey came on one night and said, "Hey, drummer, follow me and swing like mad." Jake stood up, hitched up his pants, and said "Baby I can either follow you or swing like mad but I can't do both at the same time." She walked off the show, and he got fired. I asked him why he said that, and he said, "I got tired of doing the show anyway."[15]

Roy Burns

---

15   Jake didn't get fired this time, either.

He Helped Me Make It Through the Work Day

Jim Hall

Jake had already been with "The Merv Griffin Show" for about a year when I joined the band. It was a great gig at first. I had just gotten married and it was good to get off the road, take the subway to work, and get a steady paycheck. Mort Lindsey led the band, and we had some great musicians.

From the audience looking up on the stage you could see the bandstand on your right, and on the left was a desk and chairs where Merv, Arthur Treacher and the guests sat. Merv was a good guy, he'd been a former big band singer, but we didn't have much interaction with him. We could see Arthur from across the stage and sometimes when a performer was not particularly good he'd give us these funny signals as if to say, "Can you believe this guy?"

When guests were introduced they would come out from behind the curtain, turn to their right, and walk over to Merv. One afternoon Ted Williams was the guest and he turned left instead of right and wound up at the bandstand where he stayed for a minute while he talked to us. He asked if 'so and so' was in this band, and Richie Kamuca said, "No, he's in the Johnny Carson band." We thought it was classy that he would talk with us.

After a while I started to feel that I'd gotten out of the music business because we didn't have that much to play. In fact, a few years ago I looked at the guitar I played on the show and noticed a lot of the finish had worn off where the neck meets the body. That was from the three years I spent just resting my hands on it. There were days I'd feel like I couldn't do it again, and then I'd think *oh, Jake will do something funny*. He always had something to help get us through.

Musicians would talk among themselves about why all these people would want to come inside on such a beautiful day and come into a dark theatre to watch a silly TV show. Jake created a fantasy about this mean, cruel little dog that would go outside and herd people into the show. We'd finish the rehearsal, and Jake would say, "Release the beast," and a bit later the audience would start coming in.

Merv would be in the middle of interviewing his guests when Jake would start to do his own interviews, modeled on Fred Allen's "Allen's Alley." Merv would ask a question, and we'd hear Jake muttering, "Now, wait a minute Moody." The bandstand extended out into audience, so they could see some of Jake's antics, and he'd crack them up just like he did us. When Merv had an "important" guest, two overstuffed armchairs would be placed closer to the audience for a more intimate conversation. One day he was interviewing a bishop and there was a quiet moment just as Jake chimed in 'Now, wait a minute, Bishop' and everybody cracked up.

Another time Merv had a comedian on, a young guy from Vegas—funny, but rude. He came over to the band before the show and said, "Hey, drummer," and we already knew he was in trouble. "I have a routine I do," he tells Jake, "Where I'm a cowboy surrounded by Indians. I shoot them one at a time and when I do that I want you to catch a rim shot. They ran through it quickly, Jake nailed it right away—bang, bang, bang, bang, bang—and the guy said, "Oh, you got that fast, whatever your name is." Jake said, "Oh yeah, I did that routine already for a bunch of other guys," and he mentioned several other comics. That really got the guy.

The show starts, the comedian does his routine, he's obnoxious and full of himself, and then he goes over and sits with Merv who tells him how marvelous the act was, and then he asks where he's living and the guy says, "Vegas," and Merv asks, "How's the family?" and the guys says, "Fine," and Merv asks, "How many kids you got?" and the guys says, "Three," and Jake goes, "Bang, bang, bang."

I almost fell out of my seat.

Jake was a big fan of W.C. Fields and used to do his own version of a favorite Fields' routine "The Fatal Glass of Beer." Fields would come in the door muttering, "Ain't a fit night out for man or beast," then he'd get his foot caught in a wastebasket. On the show the wastebasket was kept under my chair. As Jake got up from his seat at the drums, he had a habit of deliberately stepping into it and then he'd walk a few feet with the basket affixed as a boot. One day I poured some waster into the wastebasket and floated a few wadded-up papers on top. The rehearsal came and went but Jake didn't step in it.

That night, during the show, Jake left his drums to walk a few feet onto the stage to hit a gong. The TV cameras were rolling as he walked onstage with a very wet pant leg. The camera didn't see him step in the basket, but the band did, and they all fell out, quietly. The water had sloshed up towards his knee and Jake just had to keep on going to hit his mark and ring that gong. I did bring him a dry pair of socks.

He came to dinner one time after that and we left a plastic wastebasket inside the front door, but I don't think he noticed it.

Another time the Amazing Kreskin was a guest. He was supposed to be able to read minds, but apparently he didn't do as well with directions. To get to the dressing rooms you had to go downstairs and to the left. The band room was on the right and Kreskin kept winding up there. Jake kept telling him "Think, Kreskin. *Right* is the band room, *left* is the dressing room."

Jake was a marvelous character. I'm not exaggerating when I say he made it possible for me to go to work.

Devra Hall Levy contributed material to this section

CHAPTER
7

If it Didn't Zing it Wasn't Jake

In *100 Portraits in Jazz*, Gene Lees pointed out that jazz musicians as a group are memorably witty people, and noted that "Jake's acerbic witticisms are quoted throughout the business."

Jake was a funny guy.

No one seems to know the precise source of his humor or his exceptional comedic timing, though it owes something to his childhood love of movies. Imitations of W.C. Fields and Laurel and Hardy routines featured prominently in some of his greatest quips. His visits to the Uphams Corner Cinema provided him with a wide variety of material.

There was a humorous gene in the family that manifested itself in different ways in both parents and children. When Jim Hanna was in good form he entertained his family and friends—though mostly his friends—with his funny stories. Jake's mother Ella had a good sense of humor, "the Nichols family humor" they called it, but hers was quieter and more selective than her husband's. She would make wry observations on things she saw or read, like, "I read in the Reader's Digest that alcoholism is a disease. If so, it's the only disease that's self-induced." She and her sister Margaret often came up with pithy comments about their difficult husbands, for it was the misfortune of the Nichols sisters to each have one.

Jake and Billy were both characters when they were growing up, though they didn't really blossom until they got older. Mary Hanna Howard remembers being surprised one day in high school when a fellow told her how funny her brother was. "Jake?" she asked in surprise, since Jake never struck her as particularly funny. "No," the fellow said. "Billy." That was even more surprising, since Billy was very quiet. His humor was more like his mother's, very dry and infrequent. Jake recalled that at their father's funeral one of his cousins was talking about Uncle Jim and how wonderful he was when he came to visit and how he never drank. Billy got up and put on his coat and hat and walked to the door. The cousin asked where he was going and he said, "I must be at the wrong funeral because that can't be my father you're talking about."

Both brothers were very likeable and therefore popular with the guys. Billy's friends called him "The Chief," and when they went out they made sure to bring him along because he was so popular and people liked to be around him. It's probably fair to say that Jake had the best of his father's gregarious style and storytelling skills along with the Nichols humor, while Billy had his mother's dry sense of humor and Nichols timing. And there may have been a touch of Boston, and of Irish, too. The sisters were similarly endowed, Eleanor with her father's style and Mary with her mother's. Jake certainly honed his humorous routines in the Air Force, but he developed his own unique style that was singular, focused, and precise.

These stories come from people who knew Jake and could repeat his stories.

Whenever Jake and Denisa came to visit, my stomach hurt from laughing so hard.

Louise Sims

Jake could be caustic, but he was so funny. He was honest, truthful. Truth is the funniest thing. That's what comedy is about.

Michael Moore

The first plastic drum head came out in the mid 50s or so. Nobody liked plastic. I ran into Jake in San Francisco and we stood outside a club together while he burned the drum heads.

I loved him so much. We had more fun together.

Dick Berk

Les DeMerle showed up at the Zildjian suite at NAMM one year. He'd been playing with his big band and had already had a few drinks. Jake and I were standing at the bar when he started tapping out beats on it with his fingers — it was a portable bar by the way — then he kicked it as though it were the bass drum, then he started banging on it and suddenly he knocked it over. All the bottles and glasses went flying, it was such a mess and Jake started yelling:

"De Less DeMerle De Better."

Every year after that at NAMM, whenever Les showed up Jake would start in with that.

"De Less DeMerle De Better."

It went on for years. It became one of Jake's all time great one-liners.

Lennie DiMuzio

Vibraphonist Charlie Shoemake runs a jazz series every couple of weeks in Cambria, Calif. One time we were playing with Sam and Abe Most. We'd done a quick rehearsal, ran through the numbers, and things were going along smoothly when all of a sudden Abe said, "You know we just did a recording of Jewish folk songs. Let's play one of those." He pulls out some strangely written music and begins to conduct while Charlie and I are attempting to read this thing. After about 30 grueling seconds the whole thing just sinks to a complete stop.

From over on the drum chair Jake intones, "Drop the bow and stand away from the bass." Everybody fell out.

Luther Hughes

I heard Jake was playing in a show that featured a one-legged dancer. When someone asked what kind of a dance the guy was going to perform, Jake piped up, "The Cha."

Paul Gormley

Jake joined a table of friends after a jazz party in North Carolina, and ordered a beer. When the bartender served it, Jake pointed to his friends and told him, "While you're at it, give them a taste." The bartender looked puzzled, but did as he was told. He picked up Jake's glass and offered it around to the rest of the group.

Bill Crow

We were organizing a drum clinic with Les DeMerle across the street at the Musician's Union. I was running back and forth to set up, and at one point when I came back into the shop, Jake was there.

"Are you coming to the clinic?" I asked him.

"No, Stan, I feel just fine," he responded.

I was halfway across the street before I got it.

Stan Keyawa

There was a time in Reading, CA, when Tommy Saunders started talking about all the things he and Wild Bill Davison had in common. He said, "We had the same kind of cornet, liked the same tunes, food, etc."

Jake yelled out, "Yeah, you had the same bartender too!"

Allan Vaché

Jake was an exception among most of the musicians I worked with during the years I organized 35 tours around Germany and neighboring countries. Most of the guys usually asked about the payment, but Jake never did. He did have two questions though, whenever I called him about a tour:

"Who else will be in the band?" and " Is bratwurst and beer still available in Germany?"

Then he'd explain how his doctor told him to take three pils a day. Of course he meant pilsner.

Manny Selchow

Jake had just finished a set at a jazz festival and was heading out with some of the other guys to listen to the great Count Basie band. One can only imagine Jake's dismay on hearing the announcement that, because of illness, the great Sonny Payne would not be appearing and that Mel Torme would be deputizing for him at the drums.

Jake listened for about ten minutes and then made his way to the bar for a beer. About an hour later he was in the elevator on the way back to his room when suddenly, just before the doors closed, a breathless, red-faced (Jake's description) Mel Torme rushed in. They both stood in silence as the elevator ascended, then, unable to contain himself any longer, Torme said "OK, how did I do?"

Jake: "You really want to know?"

Torme: "Yeah, c'mon man, give it to me!"

Jake: "Well, if it hadn't been for the band ... the drummer would have fallen apart."

Roy Williams

I only had the pleasure of talking with Jake a few times but one of his comments was unforgettable: "So many drummers, so little time.[16]"

Jack Rothstein

---

16   Arlette Budwig came up with this line after her bassist husband, Monty, got stuck playing with several elderly drummers who couldn't seem to keep very good time.

Sonny Igoe had a large drum-teaching practice in NYC in the 1960s and '70s. He told of the time Jake was visiting the studio late in the afternoon on Nov. 9, 1965, the day that the East Coast power blackout occurred. They had to make their way out of the studio groping the walls of a pitch dark hallway. Jake said, "Now I know how George Shearing feels!"

Don Roberts

There used to be two Jerry McKenzies who were drummers in the Stan Kenton band, one in the '50s, the other one later in the 1960s. One of them got off the band to become a Detroit policeman. He hadn't heard Jake play before so when he saw he was going to be in town he rushed over to the club after his shift and got there just in time to hear Jake play the last tune. He was beside himself to finally meet Jake. He went up to him and said, "I'm Jerry McKenzie, I used to be on the Stan Kenton Band, it's an honor to meet you, you're one of my favorite drummers."

Jake said, "Did you say Jerry McKenzie?"

Jerry said, "Yes."

"The cop?

"Yes."

Jake said, "I always heard you had a good beat."

Jeff Hamilton

Jake said of Ray Brown that, "He plays behind the beat, behind the *next* beat."

One time Jake and Ray were playing a gig in California in two different quartets that were trading choruses. As the other group's tempo got faster, Jake leaned over and asked Ray, who was famous for playing golf, "Would you like to play through?"

Michael Moore

The story, which Jake told me himself, was that he went to see Buddy Rich after the stroke. No one but family was allowed to see BR, but Bud heard Jake in the hall and told the nurse to let him in. He *was* family. Jake walked in and said "Well Buddy, how're ya feelin'?" Buddy replied, "Jake, I can't move my left arm." Jake, deadpan, said "Now you know how the rest of us have felt all these years."

Butch Miles

Jake and I were hired to be drummers at the jazz party in Odessa, Tex. When my flight landed, the festival people said, "Oh, we're glad you made it; there was a 6.8 earthquake in LA just after your plane took off."

Jake took a later flight, and when he got arrived we asked if he felt the earthquake.

He said, "Yes, my man, I was in the bathtub."

"What did you do," we wondered.

He placed one hand over his genitals, the other over his head and said, "I just waited it out."

Jeff Hamilton

We were playing an afternoon concert in a tent, and I had asked Jake to host the session and talk about his experiences. He soon had the large audience right in the palm of his hand. It was a scorching hot day and inside the tent was like a steam bath. Everybody was suitably dressed in t-shirts and shorts but mid-way through the concert a well-known local musician arrived to hear Jake. He was probably on his way to a gig and was wearing a tux! Jake couldn't resist the opportunity. He got on mike and said, "The last time I saw somebody who looked like that he was sitting on Edgar Bergen's knee!"

Jim Galloway

At a clinic, a young man asked Jake what his favorite rock group was.

"Mount Rushmore," says Jake.

Gary Novak

There was a promoter in Scotland, Mike Hart, who no one liked. Jake once wrote an entire song parody of "Be Careful, It's Mike Hart (My Heart)." Jake was really good with lyrics.

Michael Moore

We were riding in the band bus and chipping in variations on lines from songs so that they used Mike's name: "Mike Hart Belongs To Daddy," "All Of A Sudden Mike Hart Sings," "Heart Of Mike Hart" and "I Left Mike Hart In San Francisco." It was done in good humor although I'm not sure that Mike ever quite forgave me for one of my contributions, a line from "Bewitched, Bothered and Bewildered" — "Lost Mike Hart, But What Of It!"

Jim Galloway

Jake and I were talking about Jesus and his miracles. I said that turning water into wine was one of best. Jake said, "If he had turned it into Scotch I could have gotten him a few pages in the Old Testament."

Michael Moore

Jake was playing a gig with the remarkable John Heard on bass. John is tall, black, and irrepressibly swinging, the latter attribute the only one that meant anything to Jake.

The two of them were playing an introduction to a tune, setting up a groove that brought a broad smile to everyone's face.

Jake cocked his head and said, dreamily, "Johnny Walker...."

After a pause of about a measure, their locked-in rhythm still pulsating, Jake added, "Black" — a reference to both John and the famous Scotch whiskey and its distinctive label.

The audience fell out.

Richard Simon

Jeff Hamilton hired Jake to do a drum clinic, but Jake never touched the drums, he just told stories. Someone asked him if it was OK to practice with a metronome. Jake said, "try four metronomes, all going at different speeds and then you try to play another tempo completely different from that. Because that's what reality is."

I was playing at a jazz party with Jake, and the rest of the rhythm section was a little on the sluggish side. When we came around to the last chorus I asked Jake if he wanted the bridge. "No," he said, "Because I might jump off it."

Once I was in Europe eating breakfast with Jake, and someone at our table was complaining about how expensive everything was. This person picked up a little plastic creamer and said, "I'll bet they'll even charge us for this." "Yeah," replied Jake, "But do you know how hard it is to get a cow to sit on one of those?"

Jake said, "You can tell that "As Time Goes By" was written by a German (Herman Hupfeld) because the first line says, "You MUST remember this!"

Randy Sandke

I always remember Jake's stories. In fact I tell them on my gigs but always give him credit. One of the ones I use is from the Montreaux Festival when one of the fusion jazz guys was playing and they had microphones all over the place, as many as ten on one instrument, and Jake would say they had "More mikes than in an Irish bar."

Lew Tabackin

Jake was in Japan playing with the Harry Allen Quartet when I was on tour with John Clayton. Afterwards we all went to a club in Osaka where John sat in with the trio, and then they asked Jake or me to play. I had just started eating so I said, "Jake, you do it." He gave me a look from the bar where he was drinking his Budweiser, but he got up and went over to the drums. Then a piano player at the back of the room rushes up to ask if he can play with John and Jake. And he starts playing "Battle Hymn of the Republic," the Monty Alexander arrangement. Jake keeps looking at his watch while he's playing — you can see that he wants this to be over soon — and then the piano player holds a long chord, but it's a false ending, and he starts over again and Jake yells across the bandstand, "My ace, the war is over."

Japanese interviewers never knew what Jake was saying. Terry Clarke, Jake and I were playing there once when a TV crew came into the dressing room to interview us. They asked how we liked playing in Japan and had we ever been there before.

I said, "Yes, the first time I was here was in 1984, it was a great audience."

Terry said, "I was here in 1977, and people really appreciated good jazz music."

Jake said, "Yes, I was here with a gentleman named Doolittle" — we cringed — "but I was only here for a very short time, thirty seconds or so."

The interviewers are nodding and smiling — they have no idea what he's saying — when he starts making faces and walking towards the camera. They shut if off quickly and rush out of the room.

Jeff Hamilton

Jake was doing a jingle date, and the high-handed producer was blustering about this and that. At one point he asked Jake, "Can you give me more of a . . . um, er . . . more of an Alabama-type sound?"

"Any particular town?" asked Jake.

Jim Szantor

We had a gig at a club in northern part of Switzerland called Birdwatchers Club. One night we were sitting around lamenting the lack of business and Jake said "If people don't want to come hear you play, you can't stop them."

Bill Allred

Sam Most and Buddy Rich in Chicago. A classic story.

Sam's a clumsy guy, always bumps into things and knocks them over on himself. Buddy had a group there with Phil Leshin on bass, Mike Mainieri on vibes, Wilber Wynne on guitar, Johnny Morris on piano, and Sam. Bud's got a spotlight on himself, then he tells the guy in charge, "Look, tonight we're not gonna open the same way. I want you to get some sheets from upstairs, dye them black, put a string right here, and we'll have a curtain. I want the guy with the spotlight to put a pin spot on this thing and I want you over there with the string and make the announcement and here's what I want you to say."

They rehearse it, and they do the spot and that's okay, and the curtain's okay, and they start the announcement, "Ladies and Gentlemen," and Buddy says no, he wants the voice lower. So they try it again "Ladies and Gentlemen, the Cloisters at the Maryland Hotel is proud to present the great Buddy" and Buddy says, "No, no, no, the world's *greatest* drummer," and they do it again and he wants it slower and in a lower voice, like something from a Paramount movie, and it takes an hour and a half to get it right. Finally he's satisfied. "And before this happens, I'll be doing this on the cymbal" and he plays a little riff. Then he tells everyone to be there early.

Sam shows up about 8:30, he's all set and as he walks by the other end of the bar he runs into a bunch of his old Chicago buddies and starts talking and then it's 9 o'clock, and the lights go out and it's pitch black and he hears, "Ladies and Gentlemen," and he says, "Oh, shit," he can't see anything, and the voice continues, "The Cloisters is proud to present . . . " and he heads toward the pin spot but Buddy's got his cymbals set up here and his tom-tom there — one of them has his drink on it — and Sam hits his head on the cymbal and that starts to go, and he hits his knee on the tom-tom and that starts to go, and then he goes over sideways and Bud is looking at him like *what the hell's going on* and the audience starts giggling and the voice goes on, "The world's greatest drummer," and the curtain finally opens and Bud's sitting there and the voice says, "Buddy Rich and his sextet" then Sam grabs the curtain and it falls down over Bud . . . like a shroud.

The band can't do anything, the audience is laughing, Bud is livid because he hates to be laughed at and you hear, "You're fired!" The audience keeps laughing and Bud pulls off the curtain . . . and his rug comes off. Now they're really laughing and he's yelling, "You're fired, you're fired."

Jake Hanna as told to Rory Judge

We started to play a piece by Andre Previn, and I told the story about Previn being a true child prodigy who was signed to compose film music at MGM when he was only 16. I said how he had to dash out of Beverly Hills High School and take two buses from there to get to work at MGM. From the drum chair you could hear Jake mumble, "Two buses. What a fucking idiot!"

And this one: "Frank Sinatra Jr. has a great voice. Too bad it's in his father's throat."

Charlie Shoemake

Rolling Stones drummer Charlie Watts was a friend of Jake's. Well, Jake gave Charlie a pair of Slingeland brushes that Charlie cherished and used on all his jazz gigs, until most of the wires fell out and they were no longer usable. Charlie's tech, the late Chuch Magee, had this funny idea to mount and frame the brushes like a "Gold Record" with a quote from Jake engraved on it. So I called Jake and explained what we wanted to do and asked him for a quote. I'll never forget what he said in his great Boston accent: "Charlie, these brushes look worse than you. Happy Birthday, Jake Hanna."

Needless to say, Charlie loved it!

John DeChristopher

Jake was playing with a bass player who had his amplifier up too loud. Jake finally said, "Would you mind turning that down from "kill" to "stun.""

Joe Muranyi

We were in Montreaux, Switzerland, for a Concord tour, and the organizer gave each of us a coupon book for meals. Jake loved wurst, so he collected everyone's wurst coupons and ate his way through several pounds of it.

Al Julian

I was on a Concord Jazz tour in Montreaux in 1979 with Jake, Ross Tompkins, Michael Moore, and Warren Vaché. The night before the concert, the promoter invited us all to a traditional cheese fondue dinner. They showed us how to dip the bread in the cheese and said if you lose your bread in the fondue you have to stand up and tell a funny story. Warren and I are sitting across from Jake and trying to get him to drop his bread because if anyone needs to tell a funny story, it's Jake.

After an hour and a half Jake is getting annoyed because he wants his dinner. He thinks the fondue is just an appetizer. The promoter gets up to thank everyone and just as Jake realizes this is all there is, we finally knock his bread off the fork — I think he let us knock it off — and he stands up and says, "Well, I do have one story to tell." Carl Jefferson looks at me and gives me the hand across the throat meaning he wants me to get Jake to sit down. There had been enough beer served at dinner for him to worry about any more stories being told, especially by Jake.

Jake starts in. "During WWII, a member of the RAF, a famed British pilot, is shot down over Nazi Germany," and we groan because the promoter is German. Thankfully he didn't speak English.

Carl is turning purple trying to get Jake to sit down. The promoter's girlfriend starts translating into his ear while she keeps giggling at Jake, who she thinks is so funny.

Jake continues. "Lieutenant Faversham woke up in the infirmary in bandages and the commandant comes in and says "I'm glad to zee you" " — Jake adds all the mannerisms, the clicking heels, holding a cigarette backward in hand — and the aviator says, "I hope I can get out soon." "

And the commandant says "No, no, zat von't be possible, ve must amputate your arm because it's infected."

"Oh, blimey," says Faversham, "Well, can you drop my arm over Lancaster where my Mom lives," and the commandant says "Ve vill see, ve vill see."

By now the promoter is starting to get the gist of this, and he looks pissed. He's arranged this tour and is buying dinner, which apparently is costly, and this Jake guy is giving him the business.

"Ve haf more bad news," Jake continues. "Ze ozzer arm must be amputated."

"Oh, blimey," says Faversham, "Well, can you drop it over Liverpool where me old grandmother lives," and the commandant says, "Ve vill see, ve vill see."

He comes in the next day and says "Ze arm was delivered over Liverpool, but I'm afraid ve haf more bad news. Your leg is infected and must be amputated."

"Oh, blimey," says the aviator, "Well can you drop it over Hampshire where me old grandfather is buried," and the commandant says, "Ve vill see, ve vill see."

The commandant comes back the following day and says, "I haf more bad news, ve must amputate your remaining limb."

"Oh, blimey," says Faversham, "Well can you drop it . . ." and the commandant says, "Nein, nein, ve cannot drop ze leg anywhere," and the aviator says, "Why not?" and the commandant says, "Because ve haf reason to believe you are trying to escape."

At that point the promoter slaps his hand on the table, gets up from his seat and stomps out of the room, madder than hell. He's the one paying for the festival and dinner but Jake just doesn't care. He figures if you're going to invite me out to dinner and just feed me cheese and bread, that's a problem.

Jeff Hamilton

Ray Brown was sitting across from Jake at the fondue dinner and wasn't very happy either. He kept muttering, "Fondue won't do."

Michael Moore

CHAPTER

8

Concord Jazz

Former Chicago Cubs manager Jimmy Dykes moved to Los Angeles to manage a farm team after he retired. He started taking drum lessons from Jake and they became good friends. Jimmy used to go up to Concord Calif. every three years to buy a new car at Jefferson Motors, one of the largest and most successful Lincoln-Mercury dealerships in the United States. He got to be friendly with the owner, Carl "Jeff" Jefferson, who had become interested in music in the military during World War II. His wife, Nancy, a jazz fan, introduced him to big band music, and in 1969 he established the Concord Jazz Festival. The festival became hugely successful, and Jeff then built the 8,500-seat Concord Pavilion to accommodate the crowds. Jimmy mentioned he knew a great jazz drummer and that the two of them should meet. Jake and Jeff hit it off, Jake began to play at the festival, and then invited his fellow musicians to participate.

The Concord Jazz label got its start in 1972 at one of the festival playback sessions on the second floor of the Jefferson Motors building. Jake, bassist Ray Brown, and guitarist Herb Ellis were listening to some of their performances from earlier jazz festivals and got to talking about how much easier it would be to get club gigs if they had recordings of their music. Jeff asked them what it would take to start a record company because he had a considerable amount of quality tapes that could be the foundation for Concord Records.

Jazz, one of the musical mainstays of the early part of the century, had begun to decline by the 1950s and by the 1970s it was capturing only three percent of the record business. Where a jazz album might sell 5,000 to 10,000 copies, a rock album could sell a million. With fewer people dancing to swing music and the increasing cost of travel, it became financially impractical to book big bands. Artists like Rosemary Clooney, Herb Ellis and Joe Pass could not get recording contracts. So Concord filled a huge void for Jake and his contemporaries.

The record label didn't start out as a recording company that sold its products to the public. Instead, it was a division of the Jazz Festival. Marketing and promotion was modest at first with new releases available for sale at Jefferson Motors. Jeff also had a captive audience in his customers, and anyone who bought a car got a bonus. New Mercury owners would find two records in the back seat, while a Lincoln purchase was worth a five record bonus. Concord releases became so popular that the label grew into a mail-order business and then into a record company. Eventually it required a bigger staff to handle the business and the label moved out of the car dealership.

Jeff and Jake made a good team. The car salesman had a good head for business while the drummer had the contacts to get a steady stream of artists. Their first recording was 1972's "Jazz at Concord," featuring Herb Ellis, Ray Brown, Jake, and Joe Pass on guitar. Phil Elwood, jazz writer for the San Francisco Chronicle, described it as "one of the great records of recent years, and if you're not one already, you'll become a guitar freak yourself once you're into it." For the closing night of the 1975 Festival, Jake put together a band made up of several of his Woody Herman pals, including trombonist Carl Fontana and trumpeter Bill Berry, along with Herb Ellis, Plas Johnson on saxophone, pianist Dave McKenna, and bassist Herb Mickman. The album, "Live at Concord: The Hanna-Fontana Band," was nominated for a Grammy.

Jake eventually appeared on more than 50 Concord recordings and was instrumental in bringing dozens of musicians to record on Concord, including Herb Ellis, Charlie Byrd, Barney Kessel, Warren Vaché, Dan Barrett, Howard Alden, Ken Peplowski, Rosemary Clooney, Woody Herman, Marian McPartland, Anita O'Day, and Joe Venuti.

Jake's and Carl's working relationship started to get rocky in the mid-'80s. There were disagreements over procedures and operation and they didn't always see eye to eye on the business. Then Rosemary Clooney gave an interview for a San Francisco-area newspaper in which she credited Jake for helping with her comeback and said something to the effect that he was the one who really knew what was going on at Concord Records. Jeff wasn't happy about that and apparently blamed Jake.

When they recorded "Major League" in 1986, the musicians all got baseball jerseys to wear. Jake's shirt said Hanna, with the number 0. He figured that was a message. They parted company.

These stories come from Concord Jazz staff, musicians Jake brought to Concord, and from his own interviews.

I started at Concord Jazz in 1969, before it *was* Concord Jazz, before there was a record company, before the Pavilion was even built. I worked with Carl Jefferson that very first year on the Concord Summer Festival in the park.

I remember everyone calling Jake a renaissance man, way back then. He was so knowledgeable and interested in everything — not just music — and he was so much fun to talk to. I was 18, had just graduated from high school, and was very impressionable. He could quote Shakespeare like I couldn't believe. I thought he had to be the smartest man on earth.

Ellen Herdegen

The first time I met Jake was in a studio in San Francisco where they were making one of the first Concord recordings. He was a great resource for Carl, who started the Concord Jazz label in his office in the dealership.

We saw Jake often over the years. He stayed at the house, had Christmas dinners with us and my kids loved him. They thought he was the greatest.

I'm sitting here with a grin on my face thinking about him.

Nancy Jefferson

CAD: By far your longest and most prolific association has been with Concord. You were right there from the beginning for the first three records.

J.H.: Yeah. We made the first album, that's right, with Herbie (Ellis) and Joe (Pass), and Ray (Brown).

CAD: How did the association with Concord come about?

J.H.: Through Herbie Ellis. We were working "The Merv Griffin" show together, Ray, Herbie, and myself. And the guys wanted to make a record. First time we went in there a bunch of rock and rollers tried to record us. Had all the mikes up on the tunes ... Ray leans over, he taps Joe, he says, "I don't think these guys have ever seen one of these things before." And they hadn't either. So we had 'ta have the guy do it all over, we had to have Wally Heider himself come in and do it. Imagine that. Had a sign on the shop that said, "No jazz to be performed in this studio." We couldn't believe it. It was a little hostile. And we saw why, 'cause these guys wouldn't know it if it hit them over the head.

CAD: I thought the first recording was done from the Concord.

J.H.: No, that was the second, "Live at the Concord."

CAD: Carl Jefferson was involved ...

J.H.: Yup, he was a car dealer who loved jazz. I want to make a record, got some good guys, 'some real good guys. They were operating as a duo anyway, Herbie and Joe, the duo thing started with George Barnes and Karl Kress.

Jake Hanna, Cadence Magazine

... no engineer with 32 track equipment, a thousand hours of mixing time and all the electronics and artistic skill in the world at his command can produce the sort of music that just comes naturally to a quartet composed of seasoned jazzmen in the Ellis–Pass–Brown–Hanna category."

Phil Elwood

I volunteered at the Concord Jazz Festival for several years. Then after Jeff recorded that session with Herb Ellis and Joe Pass, he decided to start a record company. He asked me to work for him, so I started part time, then went full time and stayed for 14 years.

Jake was already involved with the Festival when I started there. He and Jeff were such good friends, and Jake helped him book the artists. He was a great drummer, everyone wanted to play with him.

In all the years I knew Jake — he stayed at our house, we traveled together — I never saw him out of line. He had so many stories that would have us rolling on the floor. Once he told us about how he got picked up on a DUI in Los Angeles. He'd been out late and was pulled over by the police. He just stepped out of the car, put his hands in the air and said, "Take me away, I'm wasted." The way he told it was so funny, and he laughed harder than anyone else.

As he got older he seemed to get very health conscious and was always reading up on what was healthy and good for you. We had a garden and he liked to go see what we were growing. Whenever he came to visit I'd pick something from the garden to serve for dinner.

Margaret Glasgow

Jake was usually very mellow and entertaining at the festivals, but one year he arrived before his cymbals did, and he couldn't relax until they finally showed up.

Concord Jazz wouldn't have made it without Jake.

Lil Riley

Jake was just naturally funny. He couldn't help it. No matter what was said to him, his response was immediate, and it was witty, often sarcastic, but always with a depth of meaning.

There would have been no Concord Records without him. Or, at least, it would have been a different label. Carl was not a musician. He loved the music but did not have roots in the music world. Jake came to the label early on and became a virtual A&R man, bringing Rosemary Clooney, Woody Herman, Ray Brown and many other important artists to the roster. His "ear" and his personal contacts were invaluable.

Merrilee Trost

Jake called one day to say he wanted me to meet a man named Carl Jefferson who had just started a record company. I told him I got out of the record business because I couldn't stand it anymore, but he said I knew what I was doing and he convinced me to work with them. They'd send me a box of records and a check, and I took them around to the radio stations and tried to get them to play the Concord artists. I started part time in the early 1970s, then six or seven years later Carl and Jake convinced me to give up my "steady job" with the State of Massachusetts and work for them full time. I did their East Coast marketing for 18 years.

Al Julian

Jake had performed at the Concord Jazz Festival and was hanging around our house before he drove home.... My mom asked him if she could pack him something to eat for the six-hour drive. There were plenty of leftovers since there had been a party the evening before.

Jake looked at my mom and said, "If you would just throw me together a sandwich with lots of mayonnaise, then add some more, that'll be fine, Nancy. Thanks."

I looked down the long table and said, "Jake, you don't seem like a mayo guy."

"Oh, it's not really the flavor. It's for safety. It's a long drive."

I thought about this a moment then asked, "Safety? From what?"

"Bacteria," he said. "Mayo's a good preservative. A sandwich with plenty of it will last days."

I took this at face value but learned later in life this is entirely not true!

Tal Newhart

Jake kept telling me I should record for this company. Except for one album with Bing, I hadn't recorded in a long time. I did two tracks for the Ellington memorial album.

Rosemary Clooney, Los Angeles Times

Jake Hanna called. "Do you want to make a record?"

"You could really do almost anything you wanted to do ... just come up and make one record."

Concord (Jazz) was a label on a budget; a big band would be a bank-breaking expense. So I recorded with a small ensemble in a little studio on a side street, with Jake on the drums and Carl Jefferson listening in.

At the end of the session, Carl came over to me. "Would you like to do a record a year, maybe?"[17]

Rosemary Clooney "Girl Singer, An Autobiography"

There's no way Concord Records would exist today without Jake Hanna. Rosemary would not have been on Concord if it weren't for Jake Hanna, who had the foresight to recommend that she sing some jazz. She was touring with Bing Crosby when he suggested

---

17 Rosemary eventually recorded 24 albums for Concord between 1977 and 1998

she record on the Duke Ellington Tribute album. He got all kinds of artists to play at Concord and that was the start of the label.

Rosemary loved being at Concord, loved Jake for suggesting it, loved it when he played behind her. She had the greatest smile on her face when she talked about Jake. The two of them, with their Irish stories, it was non-stop. I remember many great times, sitting at a bar before or after a show or a session, hearing great road tales from both of them but especially from Jake. He was never without a one-liner. If he wasn't a drummer he would have been a comedian. He was a wonderful guy to be with.

Allen Sviridoff

Jake Takes Manhattan has an attractively low-key mood compared with the aggressiveness of most albums under the leadership of drummers. Jake's explanation of his philosophy clearly elucidates the reason: "Lester Young with Basie, Charlie Christianson with Benny—that's my kind of music. Such taste, such ease, such timeless music."

Leonard Feather

I met Jake in Jimmy Ryan's one night in the fall of 1976. He was doing a show with Bing and Rosie at the Uris that ran for a month, and after they finished at night the band would head over to 84th Street and hang out at Ryan's. One night the drummer there said you gotta meet Jake Hanna, he's one of the real guys, he's not like the guys today, he's the real thing. We talked a bit, then a few days later we both happened to be at Condon's very late one night and a couple of guys were playing after the regular gig was over, and I joined them and Jake loved it. He told me he knew a guy in California who would record anything he told him to. I was flattered.

Sure enough, a couple of months later Jake called and said he was sending me a plane ticket to come out to California to record on a Duke Ellington tribute album that he was putting together with Nat Pierce, Monty Budwig, and Bill Berry. Richie Kamuca had been diagnosed with cancer, and they needed a saxophone player. Jake told Carl about me and had him send me a ticket. I flew out in February.

That was my first trip to California, though it wasn't my first recording; I had been recording in New York for some small labels. But it was my first introduction to the Concord label that I recorded with for the next 30 years.

The idea behind "A Tribute to Duke" was to get a whole bunch of stars involved to raise money for the Duke Ellington Cancer Fund. Jake got Walter Cronkite, Andrew Young, Tony Bennett, Woody Herman, Rosemary Clooney and Bing Crosby together. That's how I ended up being on a record with Bing Crosby when I was 21. But the really important one was Rosemary. He brought her out, and she did two tunes with this little group that I was playing with, and the result of that was that Jake talked Rosie and Carl into doing a whole album's worth of jazz material. That really revitalized her career, gave her a whole new lease on life.

We did the Duke album early in the day. Then Carl wanted to do another record but I had to go back to New York the next morning, so he asked the other guys to stay and to play on it. I ended up making my first album "Scott Hamilton Is a Good Wind Who Is Blowing Us No Ill." The following month I came back and we did Rosie's first record, "Everything's Coming up Rosie." All three albums came out around the same time in the fall of 1977.

Scott Hamilton

Because he was so highly respected musically among the jazz cognoscenti, Jake's presence on the label added immeasurable cache and credibility. His joi de vivre and peerless skill as a raconteur didn't hurt, either. He was Mel Brooks with a ride cymbal, completely irresistible. When TWA lost my suitcase on the flight to London and I bemoaned this to Jake, he replied, "You checked a *bag* Ace? Carry-on luggage and "wash and wear" ... the greatest things that ever happened in jazz since Louis Armstrong."

Frank Dorritie

I remember Mom telling me about when a bunch of the "Concord" guys worked a cruise together and wives and girl friends came along. I don't know the details but evidently there was plenty of seasickness going around and Mom went up on deck where she met Jake at the rail. She commented that most people were staying in their cabins and Jake responded something like, "But of course my dear. There's nothing to do out here but rock, lurch and puke!"

That one stayed with me.

Doug McKenna

Jake had a story about everyone — he seemed to know and to have played with everyone — and of course he had a unique and funny delivery. He was a walking encyclopedia of the jazz world as well the whole entertainment industry.

One of my favorite records of all time is the Concord record "The Hanna-Fontana Band," with Dad on piano. Jake's on the microphone announcing the band, and when he gets to Dad he says, "Dave McKenna and the Boston Red Sox." I always smile when I hear that.

Steve McKenna

Hanna-Fontana is not a firm of lawyers, not is it a studio dedicated to the filming of animated cartoons. To make its meaning clearer, Jake is apt to refer to it as "Hanna-Fontana with McKenna at the Pianna." Jake has variously been known as the perfect small combo drummer and the ideal big band drummer.

Leonard Feather

9

On and Off the Road

After he left "The Merv Griffin Show," Jake spent the rest of his career as a freelancer. He was usually in demand and generally didn't have to look for work. "Never made a call in my life," he claimed.

He probably didn't. Everyone who needed a drummer called Jake first. And many of the vocalists did too.

He was also busy in the recording studio and made 220 of his 250 lifetime recordings between 1975 and 2009.

These stories come from people who knew and worked with Jake in his freelance days.

Jake and I were doing a drum clinic at the Professional Drum Shop in Hollywood, and we were talking about how if you really want to be a jazz drummer, you can do it. It's not easy, but if you're dedicated, you can do it.

At the end of the clinic, one guy looks a bit skeptical and says, "Let me get this straight, we can all be jazz drummers if we want it?"

"It's a matter of choice." I said. "Do you want the Bel Air mansion or the apartment in North Hollywood? Do you want the Bentley or the Volkswagen? After you've asked yourself those questions it's already too late because if you want to be a jazz drummer you don't have a choice, you've got to play the music, because jazz selects you."

Everyone applauds, and Jake's looking at me like *that was very deep, my man.*

So I say, "Take Jake, for example."

He gets nervous, starts looking at me like *whadda you mean.*

I say, "He had a house that was paid for, a car that his drums fit into, he had "The Merv Griffin Show." And he walked away from all of that to play with Oscar Peterson. None of that mattered. He had to play the music. He followed the music."

Jake says, "Yeah, and when I got off that tour I lost my house, I lost my car and I couldn't get Merv to return my phone calls."

Jeff Hamilton

In Herman Wouk's *The Winds of War* — it's a terrific book — there's a guy who goes into the Navy and becomes an Ensign and he says to his father, "Dad, I want to do just like you." And his father says, "Don't be like me, do your own work, always do your natural work. Do what is naturally you." That taught me a big lesson. The first thing I did after I read that was to quit "The Merv Griffin Show."

Someone asked me why I was quitting. He said, "The word's around town that you quit Merv."

I told him, "Man does not live by bread alone, my man. That ain't my natural work. I'm better than that."

Jake Hanna as told to Rory Judge

In `74, Oscar Peterson asked me if I wanted to go to Russia with him. I met him at a jam session on a boat, the Norway. I told him I didn't know, and he says, "I'll give you $1,500." I says, "Let's go!" I didn't get that kind of money before. So I went over to Russia. I just took a leave of absence from "The Merv Griffin Show," and I never came back.

Jake Hanna as told to Chip Deffaa

Les Tompkins: How do you find working with Oscar Peterson?

Hanna: Oh, like a breath of fresh air, believe me, after being smothered in that nonsense you have to play from day to day. It's my first time with him. I was over in Vancouver when he gave me a call. He'd been there earlier, but our paths hadn't crossed; I saw his wife up in Toronto, and he'd just left there, too. He said: "Feel like coming over?" I said: "You kiddin'? Try and stop me." He's got a sensational bass player, Niels Pedersen; they're great guys, too. Oscar is something else. He likes to have bass and drums, I guess, but actually, he really doesn't need anybody to play with him. When it comes to solo piano, there's Tatum and him. He's about the only one around today, that I've heard. Maybe there's somebody else, but I haven't heard 'em. He's just phenomenal.

It's great, you know, to be up on the bandstand with him, because sitting right there I can hear him better than anybody can. I got the best seat in the house now! I just tag along: I'm only along for the ride with him.

You don't really have to do anything; he does it all himself, and you just join in, that's all. Of course, he doesn't need no 150-pound knapsack on him. If it's not swinging — forget it.

Jake Hanna as told to Les Tompkins

So Med Flory and Buddy Clark had thought it up some time ago: "It'd be wonderful if we had a whole book of Charlie Parker stuff. But who the hell's gonna write something like that?" Anyway, Buddy gave it a shot; he'd never written in his life, but he wrote all those charts for the five saxes, trumpet and rhythm. And it's a hell of an experience—you really don't realize . . . well, a lot of people realize how great Charlie played, just from listening to the records over and over. But to see that piece of music, and hear it all the time—man, that's a heavy brain the guy had!

Jake Hanna as told to Les Tompkins

Buddy Clark and I put Supersax together. We went through some drummers — Buddy was tough on them — before we got to Jake. You could play with all the drummers in the world, but when you got to him he was unmistakable. He hit his sock cymbal (now known as a hi-hat) on every beat instead of just two and four. What tempos, he could go like crazy. He was a terrific drummer.

When we went to Japan we were there for 3 weeks before we did our final concert in Tokyo. The band was just ridiculous, we were so hot.

Med Flory

There was a guy who played drums at the bar/restaurant before it became Eddie Condon's, which Red Balaban and I owned. He was angry about being displaced and would show up drunk to threaten us with physical violence. He also had two nasty sons who were members of Hell's Angels. They came in one day when there was no one in the club but the porter, and they managed to mark up the walls and slash some of the murals.

Jake happened to come in that night and saw what had happened. He offered to contact one of his Mafia friends to have the father and sons "put away." I told him I couldn't be responsible for ordering anyone's demise but would appreciate whatever he could do to convince the guys to back off permanently.

All I can tell you is that neither father nor sons ever bothered us again.

Ed Polcer

I met Jake in 1973 when I was playing with Chuck Mangione. He would come to Donte's every night and always complimented me. I'm sure he knew that I was with Woody's band prior to joining Chuck. He invited me to the house that he shared with Dr. Deep (A.J. Kahn, though I never knew his real name) and cooked excellent pasta with shrimp.

Years later in L.A. a voice rang out from the front door of the Pro Drum Shop as I was rummaging through the used parts bin looking for odds and ends for my ancient drum set.

"What's the matter, kid? Can't you afford the new stuff?" It was Jake, of course.

We shared the stage in Seattle just after Mount Saint Helen's erupted in 1979. He was with the L.A. 4 and I was with the Bill Evans Trio. Jake wanted to know about the whacky metric modulations we used to do with the trio, so he asked Bill who told him, "I don't know what it is, you have to ask Joe." When Jake asked me I said, "I don't know what it is, you have to ask Bill," which broke Jake up.

Joe LaBarbera

I worked with Bing Crosby — now that's a different story. He's great. That's like not playing at all, when he's singing. He plays the drums for you with his singing, you know. Perfect time. Best time of any cat I've ever worked with, including Sal or Zoot or Basie or anybody. Fantastic time. He swung better than anybody I ever played with. Oh, man, and he was even better at his tempos. I don't care what tempo it is, either. "Them There Eyes," you can't have it too fast, you know... Man, he was sailing. You could go as fast as you want, and he was right on it, all the way. A whole 32-piece band, and he'll lead 'em right in. I played everywhere with him — concerts, TV shows, on Broadway — for the last two years of his life [1975–77]. He hadn't worked live in public for years before then.

Jake Hanna as told to Chip Deffaa

[At the London Palladium] Towards the end of the show, for his medley, Bing pared the band down to a small jazz combo, a fine bunch of guys; I got along especially well with the drummer, Jake Hanna.

Rosemary Clooney, ""Girl Singer, An Autobiography"

Jake told me he met Bing through Joe Bushkin who was contracting the musicians for the tour. Jake was in Donte's one night when Joe came in, said Bing was coming to town to sing live, and he wanted to get him, Chuck Berghofer and Herbie Ellis together. The Concord Jazz tribute to Ellington, which turned out to be the last recording Bing made in the U.S., served in a way as Jake's audition for Bing. They got along and then he became a part of the quartet. They hung around a little. Jake said Bing was like you or me, a regular guy. If you didn't know who he was you'd think he was a regular guy, except he's a funny guy, very non-assuming. They talked about anything. Bing loved baseball, knew a bit about everything.

Gary Giddins

I got to know Jake when I was about 17. Dad had organized an ensemble with Jake, Johnny Smith, Joe Bushkin, George Duvivier, and later Milt Hinton. They played the Palladium two years in a row and traveled around a bit, did Norway and some of the provinces.

He loved Dad and Dad had enormous respect for him.

Jake was a wonderful guy. He and the fellows he played with influenced my music. He was incredibly talented, a real liver of life, a guy who laughed at everything and always had a smile. He was a generous musician, always together. I loved his technique and his sense of time. I liked his drum kit that broke down in a special way and was very portable. He was always listening and looking and keeping great time. I remember doing the show every night in London, and then we'd steal away with Rosemary Clooney to an Italian dive in Soho and have lots of fun.

We were close during that period. It seemed like it was a long time, but it was really just a few weeks each year.

Harry Crosby

Jake was a great drummer, a joy to work with, always a spark.

I met him when we went to London with Bing. He treated us so well, and we were crazy about him, loved working with him. Jake always got a laugh out of Bing with his one-liners.

In London it was always impossible to find parking. So when Jake announced at rehearsal one morning that he had just found a parking space, everyone was surprised and impressed.

"How did you do that?" we wondered.

"I bought a parked car," he told us.

Johnny Smith

Jake knew the recitative for the majority of the songs Bing and the rest of the gang Jake would play behind. Between the Concord Summer Jazz Festival and my father's Concord Records I'd met a few drummers and found this talent surprising. When I asked Jake which recitatives he knew, he just looked at me somewhat amused and answered: "Well, all of them."

Tal Newhart Jefferson

In the late 1970s, early 1980s, there was a group called the Concord Super Band, consisting of Jake, Bob Maize (bass), Dave McKenna (piano), Cal Collins (guitar), Warren Vaché (cornet) and Scott Hamilton (tenor sax). In the early 1980s, the Concord Super Band appeared with Rosemary Clooney on a television show called "Rosemary Clooney — With Love," also the name of her newly released album.

During the program, Rosemary Clooney has a colloquy with Jake regarding a Bing Crosby tune which she is going to perform. The discussion went something like this:

Rosie: "Bing practically made every song there is popular. Jake, do you remember when Bing sang that medley of his hits in Las Vegas? There must have been 40 songs. How long did that medley take?"

Jake: "I don't know, but we were sober when we got off the bandstand."

Rosie: "That's terrible that you were sober when you got off the bandstand."

Richard Sullivan

Rosemary Clooney loved working with Jake because of his sense of humor. He played on several of the early albums she recorded and he also traveled with her. We were on a date in the middle of Ohio at a supermarket that had been converted into a dinner theater. The place was packed for the matinee, and I was waiting for the light cue that signaled me to start up the band, but it never came. Finally Rosemary's manager came out and told me and Jake to go into her dressing room. We got in there, and Rosemary said there's a tornado warning, and this is the only room that has a supporting beam. Jake calls out, "Will someone go get the wee trumpet player." We all burst out laughing.

John Oddo

I grew up in Scotland so initially I was familiar with Jake Hanna only from recordings. Then I moved to Toronto in 1964 and drove my newly acquired, beat-up old NSU Prinz to Burlington to hear Woody's band at the Brant Inn. For the first time I heard Jake Hanna in person and he made that great band swing mightily. At the time I had no idea that we were to become close friends nor that he would one day make an album with my big band.

He was the master of the one-liner on stage and off. Not all of them were original, but somehow Jake took ownership of them. If Jake liked you, it was for life; if he didn't, it was also a pretty permanent arrangement. He was straight ahead in the way he played drums and in the way he lived life.

We played together at jazz parties in the U.S. and toured in Britain and Europe.

I loved him and I miss him.

Jim Galloway

I first met Jake in 1980, when we recorded "Dear Friends" together on the Concord Records label. I also worked with him on five more Concord recordings "Swing Eiji," "Seven Stars," "No Count," "Woody Herman Presents, and "WE," which I did with Woody Herman. Then there were the records I did on my own Jazz Cook label, "Jazz Party" in 1998 and "Sketch" in 1999. He was a great drummer, really easy to work with, and we had a special connection — we were both born in April, though two years apart.

Bill Berry and I established the International Jazz Party in Los Angeles in 1991, and Jake played there each year. He introduced me to Ray Brown, and we had a great time recording "Jazz Party."

Jake enjoyed sake and had a funny way of saying in that low voice of his, "Hey, Eiji." I really enjoyed playing with him and whenever I'd do a recording I'd always do it the way Jake wanted.

I have a funny story about Jake. When he came to Japan, his fans always wanted to give him gifts. On one occasion he was presented with a wood carving packed in a big box. Jake knew it would be too big to take home with him, so he reluctantly left it at the hotel and headed to the station. But the box had his name on it, so an employee of the hotel brought it to the station. He couldn't very well refuse to take it, so he accepted it from the employee but then later left it in a trash bin at the station. As he was about to board the train, he could hear someone calling his name — "Mr. Jake Hanna, Mr. Jake Hanna, you've left something behind." Apparently an employee of the station found it in the trash and ran to find him. He ended up taking it with him to the airport, where he left it in the men's bathroom—until someone from Lost and Found saw it and got it to him. Finally, he tried to leave it at the airport when he arrived in Los Angeles, but after doing so heard his name being called once again — "Mr. Jake Hanna, Mr. Jake Hanna, your package has arrived." I've had that experience myself with Japanese fans wanting to give musicians gifts even if they are too big to carry. We both got a good laugh out of that.

Jake had lots of fans in Japan, too. When I went to play at a jazz club in Fukui (in Hokuriku), there was a big wall with the autographs of many performers. I had mine there, and about five years later I noticed Jake's name had been added. An arrow had been drawn from my name to his, where he'd written "and Jake Hanna." His name is still written there. I'll be going back to play in Fukui this fall and look forward to seeing his name there. It will feel like I'm meeting up with Jake again and remembering his interesting, playful spirit.

Eiji Kitamura

It was always a pleasure to work with Jake. I met him when he first started coming to the UK to play and we worked together at festivals and jazz clubs, in lots of different combinations in London and around Europe. And he was great company. We spent some good time together in pubs. He liked the atmosphere of the old-fashioned British pubs, the sense of history and tradition, the fact that he could relax in them. And he liked a good long leisurely pint of British beer too.

He was a very fine musician and great guy. I admired him and enjoyed playing with him.

Brian Lemon

I first became aware of Jake through his records. Then I was booked to do the 1987 Edinburgh Jazz Festival for a week as a roving bass player to fill in as needed. The Concord All-Stars were playing, and I came in as a sub for Jack Lesberg when he did other things. That was the first time I played with Jake. It was a wonderful gig, and I had a fantastic time with him. He was so encouraging and he made me feel so good as a bass player. The time was good. He was a joy to be with on the bandstand.

He came to the UK regularly, so I often played with him and Scott Hamilton and Ken Peplowski. Jake and I built up a good relationship personally and musically. After gigs we'd hang out with Brian Lemon and Roy Williams at the Nellie Dean Pub, across the street from the Pizza Express Club.

His personality is what made him so good and so funny. He took care of business but had a lighthearted attitude and was always wisecracking. He was very serious about playing but wanted to get up on the bandstand and have a good time. He had such fantastic swing.

Dave Tough is one of my favorites, and Jake loved him too. I could hear Davey in Jake's playing. I've seen that TV show of Woody Herman's and he's magnificent. It's astonishing to see him play like that, really phenomenal.

We had a lovely relationship. It's hard to put into words, but there's a certain thing with bass players and drummers. It's a bonding thing. He was supportive and uplifting to be with. If you did a gig with Jake, you knew you were going to have a fantastic time.

Dave Green

We were in Germany doing a concert after another group of musicians had played. The stage had been set up for them with the drums placed so far back that we couldn't even see them. So most of us were playing right up front at the edge of the stage, and Jake was way in the back. But as soon as we started playing Jake was right there with us.

Some drummers play too loud, and that can screw up the time. But Jake played soft, though he could always cut through to be heard.

Lou Colombo

In April 1986, Jake and I were in Germany on a combined tour with two different bands, he with one, me with another. We were staying in a hotel outside Munich, and one night we were sitting in the bar and the television was on in the background. We started to see these horrible scenes of mushroom clouds and it looked like World War III had broken out. We eventually figured out the atomic reactor in Chernobyl had blown up. The bar stayed open and we spent the night there watching and wondering if we'd even be able to get our flight home. It was kind of a panicky situation except that Jake started telling a bunch of hilarious Woody Herman stories and entertained us in his inimitable way.

Bill Allred

Our close connection with Jake started on September 26, 1992, when we recorded our first concert. That became Nagel Heyer Records CD 001, which, thanks to Jake's swinging drums, was a brilliant recording.

As Jake's flight back to L.A. was several days later, he stayed with us and used the room and bath that had been my son Daniel's. We had two dogs, and Jake was afraid that when he went home his cats might be jealous if they smelled the dogs.

Tenor saxophonist Danny Moss and bassist Len Skeat from England also had to stay at least one day longer than the rest of the band. So I took the three on a sightseeing tour through Hamburg. I confess that it was so much fun with these three guys. And I looked forward to seeing and hearing them again. We did several recordings with Jake. He was always the number one drummer whom the leaders of the bands requested. At the Jazz Parties the younger drummers always carefully watched Jake, especially the way he played with the brushes.

We all knew if Jake was playing, it would be a very swinging time.

Sabine Nagel-Heyer

When Jake first came to Germany for a tour I thought I should provide him with an exceptionally great drum kit. So I got an extra hanging tom, blockwood and glockenspiel. When he saw it he started laughing. "You don't want me to set up this shit every night, do you? Put it away!"

All he needed was his bass drum, snare, hi-hat and cymbals. But he got more swing out of this small set that most other drummers would get out of the full setup.

He was a master of the cymbals and brushes, just like Jo Jones.

Manny Selchow

Jake and Denisa were always a part of my life when it came to my father's [pianist Joe Bushkin] music. Dad would be putting his group together for different gigs, and he would always say, "Everything will be cool if I can get Jake." Then the call came that Jake would be there, and Dad would say, "Now we are going to swing." When we arrived, we would go straight to the bar. Jake and Denisa would be there, and we knew the party had started.

Maria Bushkin Stave

In the early 1980s I was flying to Sacramento for the Jubilee. Several of the performing artists were milling about LAX waiting for flights, but I lost sight of them after boarding. Later, in Sacramento, the story around town was that Jake hadn't arrived and had missed the first gig. Everyone was worried. We knew that he had been at the airport that morning, but he could not be found in the places he was supposed to be. Later I heard that he boarded the wrong plane, went to Las Vegas and had to be shuttled over for the Jubilee. This was only the first of many "Jake" stories I heard over the years as I came to know him and Denisa through my association with the L.A. Classic Jazz/Sweet & Hot Festival.

Among the many great memories I cherish was going to Jake's house for the post festival chili feast. Just being a small part of that group of luminaries was breathtaking. Names and faces that I only thought I'd see in movies and on stage were there in comfortable groupings spilling out of the house, on the patio and all around me. When I published a cookbook featuring recipes submitted by Sweet & Hot musicians and staff, Denisa was kind enough to donate the chili recipe for 500 that achieved a kind of notoriety at Jake's party.

Other people will be able to recall Jake's amazing stories and the incredible musical genius that he was, I only recall the Jake that was kind to me and — though he sometimes acted like a curmudgeon — had a great heart.

Laurie Whitlock

For several weeks in the winter of 1986, Resorts International in Atlantic City booked a group led by the great trumpeter Jack Sheldon and featuring Jake Hanna on drums. That was my first encounter with Jake, and I peppered him with questions on every break. Did he really use a bass drum cut down to five inches in depth? (He did). What was the size of his Chinese cymbal? And on and on and on. He answered every question with patience and good humor.

When the gig was over, circa 2 a.m., Jake insisted that I join him and the band for an after-hours get-together at Atlantic City's Irish Pub, which at the time was open 24 hours a day. I ordered a beer, and he asked if I ever had a "black and tan." I never had, but before I knew it, we'd all had about 10 black and tans and it was 8 a.m. What a night.

They don't make guys like Jake Hanna anymore. These were giants who would informally mentor drummers, not only about playing, but also about life.

Incidentally, I had one of those five-inch-deep bass drums made for myself after my talks with Jake. It sounded fabulous. He said it would.

Bruce Klauber

Jake was such a great player. We worked together at jazz parties and made a lot of recordings. He was a terrific storyteller and had a wonderful style. Sometimes he'd act out the stories. He was so fast.

We had this New England thing where we'd banter back and forth, especially with pronunciation. Instead of saying "potato," we'd say "buh-day-duh." We did that routine "one buh-day-duh, two buh-day-duh," and people would get such a kick out of it.

Brass players use circular breathing, like glass blowers do, so they can play without breathing. I was standing next to Jake on tour while a German group was playing. The vibraphone player played so many notes that Jake finally quipped, "He's sure got that circular breathing thing down now."

George Masso

Jake and I traveled together in a show called "Swingtime" for two months in 2000. We had a great 10-piece band and a troupe of swing dancers from England. During the show we tried several things. At one time Jake went downstage with a snare drum to do fours with the tap dancer. Now this tap dancer may have learned to dance, but he sure didn't know how to swing. In fact, every time he danced it sounded like boxes falling down steps. Jake thought it was the funniest thing he'd ever heard. Some nights he just laughed his way through his four bars.

Jake didn't like going to center stage, so eventually the band just played stop time for the tap dancer. This necessitated my conducting time, or the band would never have known when to come back in. It was hard work keeping time while that guy kept pushing refrigerator crates down stairwells. I remember Jake sitting behind those drums laughing hysterically every night. I don't think I found it all that funny, but Jake kept things in perspective for me.

He was the easiest guy to travel with. Nothing fazed him and nothing put him out of sorts. When something went wrong, as it usually does, regardless of what country we were traveling through,

Jake's constant line was, "Only in America."

That was the most aggravated I ever saw him.

I once called him to come to Switzerland for a week. He asked who was in the band, and when I told him he said, "No! Why are you working with those stiffs?"

And that was all there was to that.

Warren Vaché

It was a thrill to finally play with Jake at the PASIC 2002 concert. I'd always heard stories about him, especially from the West Coast guys who'd spent time with him before, but meeting him was really special. In the lounge after the concert, I sat with Jake and Jeff Hamilton, who seemed to drop a new beer in front of Jake every few minutes. It was a fun evening.

After listening to the '63 and '64 Herd albums, I knew practically every note on them. So to then play with him and hear how, nearly 40 years later, that "feeling" was still there ... that's exciting for a musician. Those realizations are special and remind you why you chose to be a musician.

To me, Jake was what the Japanese call a "Living National Treasure," somebody who taught us a great deal about how a drummer really leads a big band and a small band, and at the same time made you laugh and laugh. He was a real gem of a guy.

Terry Douds

I was first introduced to Jake at PASIC 2004. It was my first year working for Regal Tip Drumsticks and thus my first trade show. I was already exhausted by the end of the second day when I made my way over to meet with my bosses at the hotel bar. Jake and a few others were with them when I arrived, and somehow I found myself sitting at a small table alone with Jake. I knew of him through other people he'd worked with, and from working for Regal Tip, so I was really excited to meet him in person.

The two of us sat there for hours drinking beer and sharing stories. I didn't do much of the sharing but instead just soaked up everything he told me: how he was close to Buddy Rich, and some of the experiences they had together; how he first met Joe Calato of Regal Tip; his time with Woody Herman and Maynard Ferguson. In typical drummer fashion we also talked shop — drums, drumsticks, cymbal selection. I distinctly remember he told me to fill the sound ring on my Black Beauty snare with lead. To this day, I'm still not sure how to go about doing that.

After more rounds than I can remember, we eventually called it a night. The next day Jake performed a clinic for a wall-to-wall crowd at the show. He had everyone's undivided attention the entire time he was on stage. He was a true master of the art.

Nick Mason

One of my most memorable Jake moments occurred at our 2002 March of Jazz party celebrating Ruby Braff's birthday. Long after the music ended for the evening I wandered into one of the lounges at 3 a.m. to find Jake and Ruby, surrounded by a small circle of people, trading stories back and forth about their early days in Boston. Both were raised in the Boston area and were telling stories about their experiences working for the many unusual characters — such as Izzy Ort — who were part of the jazz scene. It was one time I did not have my video camera with me and I have always regretted it.

Mat Domber

Before I ever came to the U.S. I knew of Jake through his recordings and the videos that I watched. I admired him a lot because of the way his beautiful brushes bounced on the cymbal beat. And he played with my hero, Ralph Sutton. The two of them went so beautifully together.

Dan Barrett recommended me for the 2003 Arbors March of Jazz, and the first people I saw when I walked into the Sheraton were Kenny Davern, John Bunch, and Jake Hanna. I felt like I was in a dream!

Jake played drums on my first set, and Dan gave me a featured solo. I asked to play it with the rhythm section so I could play with Jake. And I heard, from behind me, the most beautiful thing a piano player can expect from a drummer. I was in heaven because every time I hit the syncopation he was right there with the snare drum or the cymbal, playing the same syncopation and smiling at me.

Besides being a great drummer, he was a fantastic mentor. He encouraged me so much, and encouragement means everything in this profession.

Rosanno Sportiello

The first time I worked with Jake was when we were doing a recording for Arbors Records. He didn't seem overly friendly when I introduced myself.

The most dynamic moment of a recording is the first playback, at the end of song. Jake was standing behind me when I stopped the machine, so I turned around to look at him and he said, "You know what you're doing. This sounds great. You're the man. You're my new man!" He was a different guy completely. I proved myself, and it felt great to get peer recognition. I told him, "I remember you when you were thin and had hair."

After that we became good friends, and when he was in town we'd have dinner at Fontana de Trevi. My buddy Omar was the night manager/maitre d' there. One night Jake is sitting at the bar waiting for me, and I get a call from Omar. He says, "Tell me about this guy Jake Hanna." I said, "He's a great drummer and a good friend." Omar tells me that he admired his watch, and Jake said, "Here, take it." Omar said no but Jake told him, "Take it or I'm walking out of here." To this day Omar still asks about his friend Jake Hanna, how's he doing.

That's the guy that very few people see.

Jim Czak

One of the first times I was treated to Jake's great wit was in New Jersey at the Jazzfest. I was the nominal leader of the set, and Spiegle Willcox was our guest star. I had just called a feature that didn't include the trombone. Spiegle, energetic as he was at almost 90 years of age, didn't want to get off the stage just for one number and thought it better to eliminate the extra trip down and up the stairs. So he stayed on his stool while the feature was played. Afterwards I realized I hadn't introduced him earlier in the program, so I made an announcement — "Ladies and gentleman, Spiegle Wilcox" — though of course he hadn't played the last tune. Jake said, "Yeah, Spiegle — you *looked* real good on that last number!"

I was also the nominal leader of an all-star set in Sacramento when several traditional bands were performing in the next room throughout the weekend. I wanted to feature Eddie Higgins on a solo, so I announced him, and he came to the microphone to say he would like to perform a Cole Porter medley since he hadn't heard a single Porter song the entire weekend. Jake blurted out, "I was just in the room next door and heard a guy screwin' up "Night and Day!!" The entire room broke into laughter!

I can still hear Jake's wonderful laugh. In 2000 we were traveling on a six-week tour with Warren Vaché. On the bus after a lunch break I was showing Alan Barnes a crazy letter complete with a convoluted set of directions from a bandleader who, long before e-mail, wrote through all the margins, so that the directions looked like a Jackson Pollock original! Jake overheard us laughing, and asked what we were doing. I showed him the set of directions, and between gasps of laughter he kept muttering, "Chhheeese, who da hell is this guy?!" To this day I can see Jake sitting in that seat, holding that paper and laughing hysterically.

If Jake didn't approve of the tempo that was counted, usually with good reason, he would start the intro and slow down to a dead stop like a dying battery, leaving everyone laughing. The next time it was counted, the tempo was right!

These were only a few of the happiest moments I had while I was privileged to share an all-too-short bit of the music world with the great Jake Hanna.

I'll miss him always.

Randy Reinhart

Judy Borcher and I attended the Redding (Calif) Jazz Festival the year Howard Alden took ill; Jake and Terrie alternated sitting with him in the hospital. The rest of the group had to catch a plane, the only one out of there to L.A., but Jake wanted to stay until some test results came back. Judy graciously offered him a ride to Sacramento to catch another plane back home. When Jake was satisfied Howard was out of immediate danger, we three piled in her car with Jake's trap case in the back seat with me.

We knew Jake was tired, so we let him initiate any conversation. After about 30 minutes or so of chit-chat, he fell silent. Then we began to hear what at first sounded like a faint groan. Jake was leaning forward, securely strapped in and it was soon apparent he was snoring. Quite loudly. For about an hour.

We got him to the airport, bought him some food and drink, and stayed until his flight was called. Needless to say we heard more stories and got to know him even better.

He was a special person, and I felt privileged to be among his many friends.

Bev Kennedy

Jake was a convert, a proselytizer for the shaving-cream-in-a-tube called King of Shaves. I bought my first and only tube of it on his recommendation in Denver, 2006, at Sunny's party. I have it on my bathroom sink at home. Don't use it, but can't bear to throw it out because it makes me think of Jake.

Michael Steinman

On a gig in Sacramento I was onstage with my nose buried in the music, when I became aware of someone crawling across the stage beside my drums. It was Jake peering up at the underside of my old Chinese cymbal as he tried to read the maker's name. He was very taken with its sound. I felt the same way about his Chinese cymbal, which had lost its center cup and was darned with wire so that it could be hung on a cymbal stand. He proposed a deal: whoever outlived the other would get the other's Chinese cymbal. Then he realized that any drummer who had two Chinese cymbals on a gig would never get return bookings.

Ken Mathiesen

I have been drumming for years, and though a jazz lover since childhood, I found myself in a rhythm and blues band in Britain during the 1960s. I had several hits with The Spencer Davis Group, which might not have endeared me to Jake. I played jazz throughout the last 50 years alongside many of Jake's colleagues and my first real conversation with him was a joyful experience I'll never forget.

After seeing him first live with The Herman Band of the `60s and then listening to his great recordings, I tried to catch his appearances over the next decades. I was often too reticent to try to meet him, but thankfully, my friend, Roy Williams, intervened. He had often played with the World's Greatest Jazz Band, and when I told him that they were playing in Munich, where I live, he encouraged me to go backstage to pass on his greetings to his fellow trombonist, George Masso, and the rest of that great band.

I did so easily — there are rarely barrel-chested weight lifters barring the way at jazz shows — and found myself in the catering room with the current edition of the WGJB —Yank, Bob Haggart, John Bunch, Jake, and maybe Harold Ashby, all giants and heroes as far as I was concerned. Roy Williams, a Brit, was much liked by them all and Jake offered me a Coke as my brain tried to compute my witty, humorous, and, ideally, interesting opening line for what I hoped would be a fun conversation.

Years earlier when I first met another idol, Buddy Rich, I had been warned not to talk about drums because everybody else did and it bored him. So I opened up with Robert Benchley, the great humorist, who I knew Buddy liked. This went well, and he didn't throw me out.

With Jake I was always mightily impressed by the sound of his set of cymbals and the tremendous swing generated by his playing on the ride. His magical right hand lifted any band, and I suspected I knew who one of his own idols was, another master of time playing.

"You know, Jake, I just love the sound of those cymbals, the hi-hats, the battered Chinese. They just don't make them like that anymore. Why can't Zildjian make cymbals like I hear on those old recordings of the `40s with Sid Catlett and Dave Tough?"

Little did I know but I had really pushed a button.

He practically bellowed, "Dave Tough, now there was a drummer. Buddy, Gene, Louie Bellson, a whole bunch of them, Dave could out-swing them all just with that right hand...."

There followed a glowing analysis and warm tribute to a drummer often overlooked, who died too early but left behind an essential legacy of recordings.

Jake is a giant of drumming and can be listened to on records for as long as people ask, "And what does swing mean ... ?"

Pete York

Peanuts and Chetty and Danny and Jake

Dan Barrett

The way I remember it, I first met Jake Hanna around 1979 or '80 with our mutual friend, guitarist Howard Alden. Howard had gotten the two of us a gig up in the Los Angeles area. The club might have been Carmelo's, and it might have been in Van Nuys. Howard and I were playing with a local bassist and drummer (their names lost to the mists of time), and Jake wandered in and found a seat at the bar. We knew his name, of course, but had never met him.

We played our set, and after the last tune ended, Jake quickly walked up to the small bandstand and started throwing compliments our way. The gist of it was that he hadn't heard "young" guys playing in a swing style, or actually swinging. Coming from Jake, it was of course a great compliment. We returned to the bar with him, and spent the break talking about jazz, and whatever it is that an older veteran musician talks about with two fresh, young disciples. Howard and I both recall that at that very first encounter, Jake encouraged both of us to move to New York City.

Howard moved to the Big Apple in 1982, and I followed him a year later. It changed our lives dramatically (and—I hasten to add—for the better). It was a while before I saw Jake again, but we both turned up at the long-running Midland Jazz Classic in West Texas. In those halcyon years, the party ran all week long, from Tuesday through the following Sunday. I'm not proud of how much we both drank, but if someone had to close up the jazz party's hospitality room—hosted by Dale and Nancy Hibler—with Jake in the wee hours of the morning, I'm selfishly glad that it was me! Every morning, for a week! For several years in a row! Would that I could remember specific stories and anecdotes about the hundreds of musicians Jake recalled, but I don't. I do however remember lots of laughing, camaraderie and sheer good times.

On the stand, Jake brought irrepressible warmth; I'll even say *joie de vivre*. His humor and good feeling reached both the musicians and the audience. His funny and often cynical barbs—delivered *sotto voce*, so only the band could hear—punctured holes in the most inflated, self-important players, but usually got them laughing at themselves. The impulsive one-liners shouted out to the audience—in some kind of "running commentary" about how the set was (or wasn't) progressing—would have the audience (and band) laughing so hard, it was often difficult to begin the next tune.

In 1987 (and '88, I think), Jake and I were both in clarinetist Peanuts Hucko's band for a tour of Germany. (There are several video clips of the band posted at YouTube.com). It was a good band, and we had as much fun as Peanuts—who was not a "fun-loving" guy—would allow.

One evening a close friend of mine made a long trip from Holland to see me. For a gift, he brought me a plastic bag full of loose bottles of Belgian beers and ales; perhaps a dozen or so bottles, all clanking around in this bag. I thanked him, but I soon found myself wondering how I was going to transport all of these bottles to the next town without calamity. We were traveling by train the next morning.

Well, I got myself and my trombone, and my suitcase, and the rattling bottles of beer to the station, with most of the band laughing every time the bottles clanked together in the bag. I say, "most of the band," because naturally Peanuts wasn't amused by any of it. We were having too much fun!

So, I boarded the train, stashed my stuff, and found a seat. After a bit, I decided Belgian ale or no, I simply couldn't carry all those bottles around with me. It was an accident waiting to happen. So I took the bag from train compartment to compartment, and offered each guy in the band a bottle or two of the beer for later. A few accepted, and a couple politely declined. Then I got to the next compartment, where Peanuts was sitting with Jake. I figured, "In for a penny, in for a pound," and went ahead and offered each of them a beer.

"No thanks," Peanuts grumbled.

"Uhh…no tanks, dere, Danny," said Jake. "I got too much stuff to carry myself. Maybe I'll have one wit' chu later, though."

I said "OK," and left the compartment.

Years later, Jake and I were reminiscing about Peanuts and that tour.

Jake asked me, "You know what Peanuts said after you left the compartment that morning?"

"Well … how could I know what he said? I'd left!" I said.

"Oh, yeah … well," and Jake started giggling. He finally went on.

"He turned to me, and down low—you know, confidential-like—Peanuts says, 'That Danny Barrett … I think he has an alcohol problem.'"

"Oh, yeah?" I said.

"Yeah," said Jake. "Then I said, 'I dunno, Peanuts. He seems to get all he wants….'"

I burst out laughing, and still think it's funny. Even funnier, with the stone-faced Peanuts in the equation.

It was thanks to Jake that I got to meet the great trumpeter and singer Chet Baker. In fact, it was on that same tour with Peanuts Hucko.

We had arrived into Paris early in the morning, and were scheduled to open at the New Morning Club—just down the street from our hotel— the next evening. So we had the rest of the day and evening off. Jake found out that Chet Baker's Quartet was winding up their week at the club that night. He suggested we take a nap, have some dinner later, and walk to the club and hear "Chetty," as Jake called him.

Later that night, after dinner, Jake and I bundled up against the cold: heavy coats and mufflers for us both, and me in my Irish walking hat, with Jake in the gray woolen watchman's cap he always wore.

We got to the club—just a short walk—and we could hear the loud rhythm section from the street, but even after several choruses, we didn't hear any trumpet. Jake looked in the window, and said, "Uh oh."

"What's up?" I asked.

"Looks like Chetty's missing in action tonight, man. Oh, they're taking a break. Good. Lemme see if I can find out what happened."

Just as we were about to go in, the pianist came out onto the sidewalk. I don't remember his name, but I recall he was American. Jake asked about Chet's whereabouts.

"He made the sound-check, but didn't show up for the gig, man." He took a drag of his cigarette, and blew the smoke up into the cold air. He watched it vanish, and turned back to Jake. "I just hope we get paid tonight."

Jake looked over at me. "Well, I was you, I'd just be worrying if Chet's all right, man. C'mon, Danny. We'll go get a beer, and come back later. Maybe Chet will show up. See you later, man," he said to the pianist, who nodded, puffing away.

We found a little bistro a ways down the street, and Jake talked a little bit about Chet. I remember him discussing in depth Chet Baker's great artistry and the personal problems that damaged his health and were to cause his death less than a year later. After an hour or so, we decided to see if Chet might have shown up at the club.

We got back to the club; still no Chet. On our way back to the hotel, Jake suddenly caught my arm, and said, "Oh, boy; there he is. This isn't good, Danny...."

I looked a ways up the sidewalk, and saw Chet Baker stumbling toward us. He had on a dark tweed jacket over a white cowboy shirt and jeans, and was wearing "granny" sunglasses. He was pretty messed up. He careened between the walls of the buildings and the cars parked on the street, bouncing off walls and cars like a human pinball. I felt very sorry for him.

We stopped in the middle of the sidewalk and waited a minute or so until he reached us. He managed to get his head up, and pulled it back and looked at each of us through those granny glasses. Jake smiled gently and said, "Hey, Chetty." Jake jerked a thumb toward himself. "Jake Hanna, from Los Angeles. This here's Danny Barrett. What are you doing, Chet? Are you *out jogging*, my ace?" Then Jake chuckled, not unkindly.

It took me a moment to realize that Jake's seemingly flippant remark served to set Chet at ease and passed no judgment on him or his condition.

Chet said, "Oh, Jake! Jake! Man, how are you? What a … a surprise." He looked at me, and very politely said, "Nice to meet you, Danny." I nodded and said it was an honor. It was.

Jake went on. "Hey, man! What are you *doin'* out here? You're supposed to be in there *playing*, Chet!" Jake threw a thumb over his shoulder back toward the club. "There are a whole lot of people in there who want to hear you, man. We want to hear you too. Now, come on. We'll get you a cup of coffee, and maybe you'll be straight enough for the last set.…"

Chet shook his head, and said something I've never forgotten. It was a real insight into who he was, and his artistic ideals.

"No, Jake. Thanks just the same. You heard those guys. I just can't make it with those guys. All so loud, and ugly. Man, all I want is for it to be … beautiful. I like it when it's pretty, you know? I just want to play pretty, man. But these guys, they don't know about pretty. They just want to be 'hip,' or whatever they think 'hip' is. Later for that, you dig? I can't make it. Sorry."

I was spellbound. He looked at Jake. "Nice to see you, Jakey." Then he turned to me. "Nice to meet you, too." With that, Chet Baker staggered off into the Paris night.

Jake and I watched him go. Jake shook his head. "Well, we tried. Come on, Danny, I'll buy you another beer, and then I guess I'll go back to the hotel."

We walked back to the bistro. We could both hear Chet's rhythm section as we passed the club. It was very loud, and not pretty at all.

Playing with Jake was a revelation. I had grown up listening to jazz records of earlier eras, and indeed that's where I first learned to play: along with those records.

I soon found that playing with other musicians "live" was a whole different story! When I played with my records at home, I was playing with the best! Man, I was playing with Louis Armstrong and Bix Beiderbecke, and Count Basie, and Duke Ellington's band, and small groups in the 1930s led by Teddy Wilson. I was playing with truly great trumpet players; and pianists; bassists; guitarists; and drummers.

When I first started out, many of the guys I had a chance to play with had musical shortcomings that I just wasn't used to (I'm talking high school guys here, and adult amateurs who were good enough to let me sit in with them.) Teddy Wilson didn't play bad chord changes, but many of the guys I worked with did! The bassists I played with on those recordings didn't use amplifiers and didn't solo while the rest of the band was playing. The guys I played with "for real" all used amplifiers (and "amplified" is almost always synonymous with "too loud"), and played 'way too much. There was no room left for the Swing to get in there!

Then I got to play with Jake. It was like listening—and playing with—the best guys on those records I loved! I soon discovered he was *on* many of the records I loved. Here's just one "for instance": I think every trombone player at Long Beach State University had the Concord LP of the "Hanna-Fontana" band. I sure did. Eventually, I realized that enough guys out there were copying Carl Fontana; I didn't have to be another one! So I found a different direction, which is not to say I don't have a healthy respect for Mr. Fontana's abilities. I'm proud that I got to play with him on several occasions, at various jazz parties and festivals. He was very encouraging, and of course a one-of-a-kind player (his legion of imitators notwithstanding). But back to Jake!

Here was a drummer who had the same swinging conception of time that I'd been hearing on those favorite records. It was a conception probably originated (or at least brought to some kind of zenith) by Louis Armstrong and perpetuated by those who understood his honest, swinging message. Jake was one of those, and was always quick to praise Louis whenever his name came up.

Jake was obviously influenced by the great Dave Tough ("Davey" to Jake, of course). Sometimes it was uncanny how Jake could "channel" Tough's sound and time. However, Jake loved—and had learned from—many drummers. If they swung—and played for the band instead of themselves—he loved them. Musicians come in all kinds of varieties, and there are many older cats who, for whatever reasons, won't give a younger player the time of day. Jake of course wasn't one of those. Saxophonist Scott Hamilton; guitarist Howard Alden; trombonist John Allred; pianist Rossano Sportiello; and

I are just a few of the many, many younger players who directly benefited from Jake's sage advice and encouragement. It is well-known that it was Jake who brought Scott Hamilton to the attention of the late Carl Jefferson and Concord Records (not to mention Rosemary Clooney and even Bing Crosby!) Jake was a champion for the other, then-younger, musicians I just mentioned, and many more. We all owe him a debt we can't repay.

Young or old, Jake simply dug being around guys who played honestly and who swung. Jake's tastes were guided by one's musicality and musical integrity alone. He wasn't swayed by celebrity or public opinion. Behind closed doors (usually late at night, over beers at a festival or jazz party) Jake could, and would, speak disparagingly about, say, an arrogant drummer who may have just won a magazine poll, while highly praising an as-yet-unknown young drummer he had just heard playing with a nondescript Dixieland band in the next room.

One such young drummer who Jake praised through the rafters was the great Joe Ascione, a protégé' of Buddy Rich's. Joe ("Joey," `natch) first showed up on the scene at that aforementioned Texas jazz party. That year, Jake and young Joe were the party's two drummers. Jake had the first set, and stuck around to check out the new kid on the block. Like the rest of us, Jake flipped over Joe's technique; his understanding of the various song forms; his fluid time; and his overall conception and sound. Of course, Jake had been—along with Buddy Rich and a short list of others—one of Joe's heroes long before this in-person encounter. They quickly formed a bond that lasted until Jake's death.

I had a singularly odd and memorable experience a couple of years ago. My friend Chuck Redd invited me to join him for a weekend at the terrific jazz club, the Jazz Corner, on Hilton Head Island in South Carolina. Chuck played vibes that weekend. (He's also a very good drummer.) Nicki Parrott was the bassist; Chuck's brother Robert played piano; and Joe Ascione was the drummer.

On opening night at the club, we began the first song of the first set. (I can't remember what it was, but it doesn't matter; some swinging thing.) At the end of the first chorus, Chuck turned to me to play the first solo. I came in feeling good, and suddenly the hair stood up on the back of my neck! I was playing with Jake Hanna!

I finished my solo, whirled around, and saw Joe smiling up at me. He knew exactly what I was thinking, and wore kind of an evil grin. He pointed a stick at the high-hat cymbals. I recognized them immediately; they were Jake's! To hear them behind me again, played by Joe with an authority and "lift" that was uncannily similar to Jake's own playing—was just too much. I wanted to laugh and cry at the same time.

Jake had often told Joe that those special cymbals would be Joe's "one day." That day sadly finally came, but those cymbals couldn't have gone to a better guy or more deserving drummer. It was nice to hear Jake—by way of "Joey"—one last time.

10

Uncle Jake

Jake's three uncles only had eight Hanna and Nichols nieces and nephews to keep straight.

Jake had 16 Judge, Howard and Ruff nieces and nephews he doted on, though his performing schedule didn't usually allow for frequent visits. In the late 1950s while touring first with Toshiko and later with Marian, he visited his sister Eleanor's family in South Bend. After his move to New York, he would visit his parents and his sister Mary's family when he came back to Boston. Once he moved to Los Angeles, he didn't get back to Boston as often, but in the 1970s, the nieces and nephews became old enough to start visiting him.

The 21st century was filled with visits, especially at the jazz festivals and parties where Jake performed, and at the occasional family wedding. He got back to Boston more often for reunions of his old neighborhood gang, and there were visits to Colorado to visit his youngest nephews, Chris and Drew Ruff.

The following stories come from the nieces and nephews.

Jake was very proud of his nieces and nephews and always talked about them (and his sisters) when he stayed with us in Boston. Family was important to him.

Anna Julian

When I was little I knew my uncle was a drummer, but I didn't really know what that meant. When we went to the movies, just before the feature started, they used to show a cartoon clip of drum music with a close-up of cymbals, and I always asked, "Mom, is that Uncle Jake?"

Peggy Howard Solari

In high school I was a "band fag" (no offense intended; that was what we were called). I quite enjoyed playing, despite my limited talent. Mr. Evans, my band director, assumed my minor piano experience would lead to a career playing the glockenspiel or xylophone. He was wrong.

One of my fellow band members was the very talented saxophonist Bob Bowlby[18]. One day I told him my uncle was a professional drummer, at the time playing for Merv Griffin. He jumped up and yelled, "Mr. Evans, Mr. Evans! Do you know that Jake Hanna is her uncle?"

`Twas then I realized Uncle Jake's name held power … and mine did not.

Mimi Howard Zakarian

The first time I met Jake when I was playing in Stockholm in July 1986 with Buddy Rich. We did an afternoon TV show on a boat and Jake came by to see us play. I introduced myself and told him I grew up with his niece Mimi in Milton, Mass. We hung out most

---

18 Bob Bowlby later went on to play with the Tommy Dorsey and Artie Shaw Orchestras and with Buddy Rich.

of that day and evening into a late night jam session at the Castle Hotel. We were friends from then on and used to run into each other at airports in Europe going to and from gigs.

Bob Bowlby

I was also in the Milton High School band, but was a bit rebellious. One day I was being disruptive, so Mr. Evans kept my friend and me after school. We were utterly bored and finally I said "Mr. Evans, do you remember Jake Hanna?"

"Yes," he said.

"Well, I'm his niece," I announced.

"No you're not," he said. "Sit down."

"If I bring you proof, if I bring you a record tomorrow, can I go?"

"I don't believe you, but go ahead. If you don't bring me an album tomorrow, you'll be in detention again."

So I swiped an album from my mother, brought it in the next day, and got out of detention.

Joan Howard Fitzgerald

Uncle Jake sent us a box of Christmas presents when I was in the 8th grade. I don't remember what anyone else got, but he sent me a Polaroid Swinger camera. I thought it was one of the best presents I'd ever received, and I couldn't believe my good fortune.

Neither could my friend Bunny who, as she gazed at it, must have been thinking of the presents her family got from their uncle, Father Dick.

"Gee," she said. "It's more fun to have an uncle who's a drummer than an uncle who's a priest."

Maria Judge

We knew that our next-door neighbors, the Judges, had a famous uncle who was on television, and we also knew they didn't have a TV. My mother used to watch "The Merv Griffin Show" in the afternoon and when we heard the opening music we'd run outside and yell "Hurry up, your uncle is going to be on, it's time for Uncle Jake," and all the kids on the street would run into our living room and we'd watch the beginning of the show and when we saw him we'd yell, 'There he is, it's the Judge's uncle!'"

He came to visit one summer and we all crowded into their living room for a jam session one afternoon. Jake played Rory's drums and Mr. Judge played the piano and we all danced around the room. It was so much fun.

He was always such a pleasant guy, so friendly, with such exuberance for life. He went out for walks all the time and when he saw me he would say, "How you doin' there, Patsy?" I didn't let many people call me Patsy but it was okay for Jake to do it.

Patty Tierney Belforti

Jake, Denisa, and I went to Disneyland to hear Buddy Rich, Toshiko Akiyoshi, and the Duke Ellington Band, among others, play in the various pavilions. It's kind of strange to think of Jake in Disneyland, but I understood from Denisa that wasn't his first time. He'd apparently been there once when Walt Disney himself showed up, but that was before my time.

They stopped by my apartment in Orange County to pick me up. When I ushered them in I asked them to take their shoes off, Japanese-style, but Jake would have none of that.

Valentina Judge

Back in the mid 80s, I was on the road with NRBQ (New Rhythm and Blues Quartet) when Mum told me Jake was playing in New York with Woody's band. My then-girlfriend, now-wife, Liz, and I took the train into Manhattan, checked into a hotel, and headed out dressed in the clothes we wore for the "Q." Woody was playing at the St. Regis and the Beefeater guards at the front door only added to the chill of the evening with the look they cast upon our rock and roll finery. Liz wore ripped jeans and a leather jacket with a fur collar while I was nattily attired in a leather jacket, ripped jeans and sneakers. Ours were the only ripped jeans in sight. The rest of the jazz fans wore suits and fancy gowns.

The maitre d' wanted security to remove us, but we begged him to call Jake, who took one look at us and shook his head in disgust. After a lot of haggling and swearing, some of it directed at us, we were led to a booth where a busboy unscrewed the light bulbs over the table. We watched the show in complete darkness, hidden from the other guests. It sure was an eye-opener into Jake's world. He did come and talk to us briefly afterwards; he wasn't proud of us.

It's a funnier story now than it was back then.

Andrew Judge

———————————————

I was living in Nashville when Jake came there for PASIC 2005.[19] My brother Rory and I got to the Convention Center and found Jake at the Regal Tip booth, signing autographs on cymbals, drumsticks, old LPs and more. I was awed by how young some of these kids were — one just 11 years old — as they waited patiently in line to get his autograph. Their grandparents probably knew of Jake, yet his legend was still so huge in the percussion community that little kids wanted to get his signature.

That night at the dinner and awards show we sat with Jake and the Calatos, of Regal Tip Drumsticks. Rory pointed out people of interest and I realized that, although neither Jake nor Joe Calato was much taller than 5 foot 5, they were the giants. Lots of folks came by to pay homage. The wine flowed, the dinner was wonderful, and I didn't want the night to end.

The next day Jake was holding court at a Master Brush class, but we didn't know which room it was in so we wandered around until we got to one of the last ballrooms. There was still no sign

———————————

19   The Percussive Arts Society International Convention

of him, but we knew this was the room because it was already packed, standing room only. We leaned against the back wall until Jake showed up with Joe Calato and his wife. I waved them to two seats, but Joe pointed out that they already were occupied. I replied, "You're Joe Calato, you sit where you want to sit!" The two occupants of the seats responded promptly and gladly offered their seats to Joe and his wife, both of whom were laughing. Anyone standing in Joe's line of sight was tersely reminded that, "Nobody stands in Joe Calato's way." Everyone was a good sport, and the crowd found this whole thing very entertaining.

Meanwhile the drum clinic turned into a combination of master brush work and Jake stories. He wrapped up by roasting Jeff Hamilton, who laughed so hard he had to leave the room. [20]

That night we went to the Nashville Jazz Club to hear The Jeff Hamilton Trio. People started applauding lightly as we walked in, and I looked around for the big name in the room, forgetting who I was with. I was surprised they didn't have a bar but people brought their own booze and kept coming by to make sure "Jake and his nephews" never had empty glasses. Then Jeff pointed out that Jake was in the audience, and the place erupted in applause. They set up another snare drum, and he and Hamilton performed an impromptu version of "Salt Peanuts," and the place went nuts.

I was floored by my uncle's reach and all the people he'd touched. I didn't want the visit to end.

Jerome F. Judge

Uncle Jake christened me "Jackson" when I was still in the crib, and "Jackson" I remained.

Every few years I'd call the house, and he'd ask, "Jackson, are you at the airport?" and I'd say, "No, I'm home on the couch," and he'd ask, "When are you coming out?"

---

20   Jeff reports that although he was laughing, the reason he left the room was to get ready for his own drum clinic.

Then we'd talk about the Celtics and the Patriots. We always talked a lot of sports.

When I was 25 I drove cross country and stayed with Jake for a couple of weeks. He took me to a jazz festival, and I had a great time listening to the music and hanging out with the musicians. I'd start to feel uncomfortable when he began telling stories that weren't exactly complimentary and the subject was standing right there. But soon a rebuttal would come back and Jake was the punch line.

I had great admiration for my uncle. He loved his work, he loved life and travel. Through his stories and his life lessons I came to consider him a very wise man.

Jack Howard

Jake Hanna wasn't really my uncle, but Rory Judge and I met in the 1st grade, and I spent a lot of time at his house, and he talked about Uncle Jake often, so I started to feel like we were related. I met him once in the 1970s when Rory and I went to hear him play in Boston, and I began listening to his music. I didn't see him again until 2005 at the Sweet and Hot Jazz Festival.

Rory convinced me that it would be a great swinging time and that most of his family would be there, so I decided to join the crowd. I was one of the first members of the "family" to get there and after checking in I went downstairs to the ballrooms where the performances would be held. It was early, and people were still checking in. Most of them seemed to be around my parents' age, and there was an assortment of wheelchairs and oxygen tanks, and I started to wonder what that Rory Judge had gotten me into. I went back to my room to see if I could move my flight up a day so I wouldn't be stuck all weekend in this place.

Then the music started. And then I heard Jake play. And then I sat next to Jake at dinner. And then Jake started telling stories. And then we started choking on our beers. And then I tried to move my flight back a day so I could stay until the very last song was played.

Scott Thorburn

Uncle Jake was our favorite uncle because he was so funny and sent the best Christmas presents. I never realized how famous he was. We just loved him because he was such a great guy.

My brother and I went to visit him and Aunt Deni. Jake had a toothache and was on pain medication that made him feel a little out of it. One afternoon I was playing video games while he was sitting in his underwear in his favorite chair in the living room. I asked if he would rather watch TV, but he said no, he liked watching me play.

Now Jake had a fondness for ice cream. He really loved Drumsticks, and Denisa stocked up whenever we came to visit. She went to work that day but told Jake he had a two Drumstick limit. At one point he went out into the kitchen and returned with four or five of them, then sat there watching me play the game, the point of which was to kill zombies.

"Get 'em Drew, get 'em, yeah, get 'em," he was calling out to me. He was so enthralled by me killing zombies.

He showed so much love for everyone. I especially noticed it with his pets. He had a huge fish tank and when it was his turn to feed the fish, he fed them way too much so they almost exploded. He made fish faces and talked to them. He loved his cats; he'd sit and play with them.

I received the greatest compliment when I told a story at his kitchen table and he said, "Drew, you're a funny guy, a funny guy."

That's the best comment I've ever had from the funniest guy I ever met.

Drew Ruff

I'm Nobody, but my Uncle is Jake Hanna

Rory Judge

As a young child, I remember watching my uncle Jake on "The Merv Griffin Show"—at least I did when we finally got a television, and on those rare occasions my parents allowed us to watch it. We had his records, and I know that listening to them was the major influence on my wanting to play the drums. I bought my first drum set when I was 10 years old, a blue kit that I ordered from the Sears catalog. I played in the school marching, symphonic and dance bands, and spent all my time in the music room—at least that's what I told my teachers.

Although I grew up listening to The Rolling Stones and The Beatles, I also listened to the big band drummers of Woody Herman, Count Basie and Duke Ellington. It was because of Jake that I became aware of that kind of music, but none of my friends listened to it or even cared about it. It wasn't that easy for me to find out about those great drummers. Today a kid can go on YouTube to see and hear them.

Jake sent me my first real drum kit when I was about 14. It was the first wood and fiberglass set made by Pearl Drums —I think he was endorsing them at the time. He told me he had used that kit briefly and then shipped it to me. I was so proud of those drums, and I still have the bass drum today. It weighs a ton.

Jake gave me my first real drum lesson when I was about 15. It took place in the living room of our family house in Hull, and we used the drum set that he sent me a year or so earlier. The whole neighborhood came to watch. We concentrated on the cymbals and the swing beat (of course). He showed me the correct way to say it, the correct way to play it, and the many ways drummers mess it up by playing it wrong so it didn't swing. He kept driving home the point of how you had to do it right and make it swing. It was a lot for a 15-year-old rock `n `roll wannabe drummer to comprehend, but I never forgot it. I still practice it and one of these years I hope to have it down.

After he finished telling me what to do, he said, "Show me what you got." I played what I knew, as loud and as fast as I could. The kids clapped, and I felt good and then Jake sat behind the kit and proceeded to copy exactly what I had just played, but he barely moved his arms, and he made funny faces the whole time. It was a very funny and humbling moment.

But he never really gave me formal lessons until just a few years before he died. The rest of the time he showed me how to do things on a tabletop or more often on the top of a bar while we were having a drink. He would show me things he had learned from Buddy or Gene or one of his favorite drummers, Jo Jones. He would beat out a pattern with his hands and explain what he was doing and then tell me to figure out how to apply it to the hi-hats or cymbals.

Most of his lessons were about cymbal work. Many have said that Jake was famous for his brushwork, and while that may be true, his cymbal work was really amazing. He could do so much with just a few cymbals, could move a whole band in any direction just by hitting an accent on one cymbal and switching to another for the next section of the song. To me, his cymbal playing is subtle yet powerful, simple yet intricate, and totally mesmerizing, all at the same time. Something happens when his sticks hit the cymbals. He showed me how he holds his sticks and exactly where to hit the cymbals, but when he does it, the sound is like nothing else.

Charlie Watts of the Rolling Stones told me that he once saw Jake at a club before anybody else had arrived. He stood by himself at the back and just watched him hitting his cymbals. He had never heard a sound like that before. "Nobody plays like that!" he told me.

I was exactly 50-years-old when I first got to play those cymbals. Jake and Denisa came up to San Francisco after the Monterey Jazz Festival, and I happened to have a gig with a six-piece jazz band on the night of my birthday. Jake let me use his cymbals, sticks and brushes. What a thrill. I remember hitting the hi-hats for the first time and thinking *I have never felt anything like this before.* It was a great night, and even though he wasn't feeling so good (it was about a year before he died), he got there early to hang out and talk with my friends. He even sat in with the band. They couldn't believe they were playing with Jake Hanna. It was a real treat for everyone.

I listened to a lot of rock `n `roll drummers when I was young, but Charlie Watts is the only one I still listen to today. I knew Charlie loved jazz and I hear it in his drumming style. Jake told me that Charlie used to come see him play when he was with Woody in `64, and they kept in touch over the years.

Around 2005 the Stones were playing in San Francisco, and I told Jake I thought I'd go meet Charlie. Jake was all for it and said, "Tell him I said to keep swinging." I was able to get word to Charlie that I'd like to visit him, and got a message that tickets and a backstage pass would be waiting for me. It was almost time for the band to go on when I got to the backstage lounge and the fire marshall was clearing out the room. I managed to squeeze through the crowd and made my way to the back of the room where I saw a familiar face, the longtime road manager for the Rolling Stones. He told me to leave or get thrown out. As security bore down on me I quickly explained that Charlie was expecting me, but he still told me to leave. So I asked him to show me the way out, and by the way, could he please tell Charlie that I had stopped by. He gave me the once over and asked, "Who are you?"

"I'm nobody," I said, "But my uncle is Jake Hanna, and Charlie invited me here."

"Stay here," he told me. He disappeared, then returned quickly to escort me to Charlie's dressing room.

Charlie welcomed me warmly, and we had a brief but great chat about Jake and jazz drummers. His love of jazz was so apparent, and he had lots of questions about Jake. We talked for a while, and I gave him a pair of Jake's brushes that he had used with Bing Crosby 30 years before. Charlie told me

Jake sent him a pair of brushes many years earlier and he had them hanging at home, framed. He was very happy to accept my gift. (I should point out that I had two pair of those brushes; I was not going to give away my only pair, not to Charlie or anyone else.) I was able to see Charlie and his band many times over the next few years, and he always got me as many tickets and passes as I wanted.

In March of 2006 I arranged a dinner at Jake's house in LA for Charlie and his good friend Jim Keltner, who Jake referred to as "a true artist on the drums." It was an evening to remember. Denisa served up a drummer's feast of fabulous homemade minestrone with bread and wine, and we sat around the table in the kitchen for almost four hours listening to stories about legendary jazz musicians and great drummers. There was lots of laughter, a little craziness, and a beautiful connection between two generations of great drummers. At one point Jake pointed at Charlie and said, "Charlie, you are a rock `n `roll drummer who swings."

It was such a comfortable environment at that table. It felt normal, like old friends sitting around sharing great stories and memories. I felt lucky to be included, and Jake made me feel like I was one of them. But really, I was sitting at the table having dinner with three of the greatest drummers of all time. When the evening was over, they all signed a drumhead—I don't remember who asked for it, but know it wasn't me—and talked about getting together again.

Six months later, we were all back at Jake and Denisa's dinner table again, and this time was even better. There was talk about making "Dinner with Jake" a regular event. Sadly that was not to be, but I will never forget those two amazing evenings.

That drumhead is framed and hangs on my living room wall along with a photo I took that night of the three of them. Jake signed it "Keep Swinging."

Chapter 11

Generous Jake

*J*ake always had time, and advice, for people he thought worth encouraging. The following stories come from some of the recipients of his generosity.

I liked to sing when I was a kid, and I won an amateur television competition called "You Want to be a Star." After that I started singing but would get really nervous before I had to go on.

Jake would say to me, "It's okay to be scared, all the good singers get scared."

He was always nice to me, always interested in what I was doing. I was flattered by his interest because he was older.

Jim McCarthy

When Kenny and I were first dating he took me to the Village Vanguard in New York City. I already knew a lot about jazz but didn't know any other jazz musicians personally. Zoot was playing that night and Coleman Hawking was sitting in a corner. It was overwhelming, smoky, there was lots of action. Jake was also playing and he came over to our table before he went on; he was charming, full of witticisms. He looked at me and asked, "Are you all right?" I said, No, I feel a bit dizzy." He turned to Kenny and said, "Take her home." I never forgot his sensitivity at that moment. You could tell from his playing that he was a sensitive man.

Elsa Davern

Jake called one day shortly before Christmas 1971.

"I just bought you a car. Why don't you and Jerome fly out and pick it up."

Just like that.

Jake knew this guy who had the car shipped from Germany, then decided to move back and didn't want to take it with him. He asked Jake if he knew anyone who'd be interested in it, and Jake decided to buy it for us.

At the time our family station wagon was being held together with rope — literally, since one of the kids got into an accident that warped the back passenger side door, so the only way to keep it closed was to tie the doors together with a rope that ran across the back seat. The idea of another car was appealing.

Jerome and I flew out the day after Christmas to discover the car was a champagne-colored Mercedes-Benz. Perhaps not the most practical car for a family of 11, but it certainly was beautiful. Jerome couldn't wait to get his hands on it, and neither could Jake's housemate, the Doc, a real character and a big jazz fan who took us out to several clubs.

We had a great visit, saw the New Year in with Jake, then I flew home on Jan. 1. Jerome planned to head out the following day with the Doc who was going to visit his family in Athens, GA. Jerome couldn't wait to get his hands on the car, but neither could the Doc. So Jake and the Doc spent the evening pouring Scotch down Jerome, who fell sound asleep and didn't wake up until somewhere in Texas where the Doc stopped to visit his friend Van Cliburn. He didn't get his hands back on the steering wheel until after the Doc got off in Athens.

Eleanor Hanna Judge

I remember Jake coming to the house when I was a kid, and we'd talk about baseball. He'd tease me about my batting average.

He always made an effort to talk to me when he came in to the shop. Not many of the other guys would do that.

Tom Yeager

Jake called me up when I was with working with Buddy Rich and said, "Whale, we have to get Sam Woodyard a ride. He needs to get out of town."

Sam was a great drummer but he was an alcoholic and Jake figured he'd get into trouble if he stayed in L.A. with no work. Jake asked if I could get him a ride back to New York on Buddy's band bus. Buddy said, "Not only can he come on the bus with us, but let's put him to work." He told me to pick up some congas and when we got to New York he recorded an album with us. Jake engineered the whole thing, got him on the bus, made sure he had some money in his pocket, and made sure I sent some of the money to Sam's wife in Boston.

Charlie 'the Whale" Lake (Kaljakian)

Jake Hanna gave me advice the very first time I met him.

I was a freshman in college, about 18 years old. I went into Eddie Condon's one night and sat down at the bar between Tommy Flanagan and Jake Hanna. Jake was one of my favorite drummers and was on one of the first records I bought. In fact he probably was on half of the first 50 records I bought. I would always look at the list of musicians on a particular record and pick out the ones that featured my favorites.

I said, "Mr. Hanna, I'm such a huge fan of yours."

Before I could continue he said, "Listen kid; let me give you some advice. Get yourself a metronome, but set it at a different tempo than you're playing at, because in this business you're always working against people, never with them!"

That's a very funny thing to say to a musician; why would you ever set it at a different speed than you're playing? You have to have your own time feel and be able to impose it on a band when it's called for. It was a funny comment, but he was right. Most of my favorite musicians are the ones who do that with their time, who impose it on the band they're playing with. Jake was exactly that kind of drummer. That's one of the things that made him so great. He and Ray Brown and Charlie Parker and Ben Webster, they all did that.

I think the first time I officially played with him was in 1990. He was always supportive and complimentary. He said I was one of his favorites, so I know he helped behind the scenes to get me gigs.

Another thing that fascinated me was how, at jazz parties with just one drum set for all the drummers, Jake got such a wide variety of sounds out of it, in a way that others couldn't. He made me realize you could also do that with a saxophone, widen the variety of sounds from it.

Jake was funny on stage, particularly at jazz parties where it was more relaxed and not so serious. But I will always remember one evening at a gig in Half Moon Bay, Calif. Jake and I were play-ing in a quartet with Ross Tompkins and Dave Stone. Jake was very serious, he wasn't saying or doing anything funny. He was playing like he played with Woody's band, with an unbelievable intensity that you didn't hear at jazz parties. Dave and I spoke afterwards and asked each other, "Have you ever heard anything like that?" "No, have you?" It was more like a concert atmosphere.

Jake had a very profound effect on my career, musically and also business-wise. I loved his playing, and I loved playing with him. I got to work with him a lot, and it helped me enormously. But it was his attitude of 'the only thing that mattered was swinging," which was the way he ran his career. That was really an example for me. He'd say, "If the gig isn't swinging, get me off it." And that's how I've tried to handle my career, by following Jake's path.

Harry Allen

My first "meeting" with Jake Hanna was hearing him on a Woody Herman record when I was in high school. A friend gave it to me and told me to listen to the drummer. Jake's playing was beautiful from start to finish. His time feel had such great forward motion, and was full of such life that I still use his playing on tunes such as "Caldonia," "After You've Gone," and "My Funny Valentine" as examples for students.

His playing made an enormous impression on me, and it was a real thrill to get to meet Jake a few years later. His playing matched his personality. He loved life, people, and swinging music. And he loved to laugh and tell jokes. His sense of humor is the stuff of legends, and I love to hang with friends who were fortunate to know him and tell Jake Hanna stories.

Early in my career I was on a jazz cruise with Woody Herman's band, and Jake was also playing the cruise. Late at night you could find him hanging at the bar, holding court, telling stories with friends. The funny stories and the witty comments are all the stuff of legends. I went up to him one evening and asked him a brush-playing question. There was a certain tempo that I had trouble getting the feel to swing, and I asked Jake what he did. I expected some words of wisdom from a master, but all he said was, "Oh, I always play sticks at that tempo!"

In 2002 we did a tribute to the drummers of Woody Herman at a Percussive Arts Society convention, and the lineup was impressive. We had Jake, Ed Soph, Joe LaBarbara, Steve Houghton, Jeff Hamilton, and John Riley — all these guys are world-class drummers. The first guy to play at the rehearsal was Jake, and when he played the intro and head to the "The Good Earth," all riding on the hi-hats, I think he schooled us all. We were standing along the side of the room listening to that amazing sense of time and energy. I shall never forget that feeling.

I will always remember Jake telling me that he was at the stage in his life where he just wanted to play music he liked, with people he liked. He seemed to have succeeded in that area.

Jim Rupp

Jake was very important to me. So many things happened because of him.

He was the one who brought so many of us to Concord and got us touring. I was twenty one years old and very impressionable, but I could talk to him about anything. I was very much into Jake's style in those years — we both liked Gene Krupa. I talked to him all the time. He didn't give me advice directly, but I could go to him and say, "Jake, I've got a problem, what should I do?" He would sort of tell me without really telling me. I learned a lot of things from him. There were times when I was young and not very proud of myself, walking around wasted and out of it, and I could hear him telling me to clean up my act. He had a very strong presence.

Working with him was amazing. He was a dream to play with, one of those drummers who paid attention. He was always there, easy to work with. I know that he didn't like to work with people he felt weren't up to his standard. He would only do things that were 100 percent good so sometimes he didn't work for months on end. It might have been better if he could compromise, but that's just the way he was. In the early years when I knew him he was doing all sorts of gigs, he was a pretty busy guy. He would complain about some of the gigs, but he enjoyed playing and wanted to play. He always wanted to know who's on the gig and he'd say, "Oh, so-and-so is on the gig. I'm not working with him."

He was ahead of his time in a lot of ways. He was the first guy of all the studio musicians that were working in television to walk off a major television show because he wanted to play jazz. Of course, he had low overhead, he wasn't even married then. But it was still a brave thing to do. More guys walked off later when they saw he could get away with it.

He didn't suffer fools, didn't have time for it. Television started turning into one silly situation after another, and that wasn't for him. He felt he'd done enough of that. He didn't get himself tied up the way a lot of guys did with expensive cars, expensive houses, expensive ex-wives, or children to send to college, so he was free to do a lot more than other guys who were in no condition to quit anything.

Jake was his own man.

Scott Hamilton

Jake Hanna inspired me to pick up a pair of drumsticks and play music.

In 2001 I watched a video of him playing "Perdido" with Scott Hamilton, Warren Vaché, John Bunch, Bucky Pizzarelli and Jeff Fuller. I was amazed by the fluidity and fullness of Jake's playing and by how strongly he supported his fellow musicians. When it was his turn to take an extended drum solo, it was obvious how the other musicians respected him as they turned around on the bandstand and gave him their full attention. He played on the cymbals and moved around the drums with ease. Jake built his solo, and when the band came in for the final shout chorus, played fills to propel the band to the end.

I watched him and knew I wanted to be a drummer.

In my early days, what struck me most about Jake's playing was how he set the beat, regardless of venue, stage set up, or instrumentation of the ensemble. He was a great role model, and I learned countless lessons from listening to his recordings: the importance of always being prepared; keeping good time; playing at the highest level at all times; and supporting other musicians by not playing too many notes but then giving everything you have during drum solos.

Although I never met Jake or heard him play live I am fortunate to have known and played with three great musicians who did. Eddie Higgins, Lou Colombo, and Dick Johnson are featured on at least one recording with Jake. I loved to hear them talk about how Jake had the highest musicianship on the bandstand and the greatest personality and sense of humor offstage. They explained how Jake's sturdy sense of time helped any band he played in to swing, and how his stories and jokes lightened any mood and created an atmosphere where all the musicians performed to their maximum potential. Playing with them and hearing their stories made me feel the spirit that I think was also Jake's.

Now, when someone asks me, "What is swing?" I answer, "Jake Hanna."

Kareem Sanjaghi

When I was young I woke up in the middle of the night to loud voices and laughter coming from the first floor of our home in Niagara Falls, NY.

I snuck downstairs to see my mom in the kitchen cooking pasta for a group of men who were sitting around talking music. What I didn't realize at the time was the significance of this night. My dad, drummer Joe Calato, had gone to see the Woody Herman band to introduce his new nylon-tip drumstick to drummer Jake Hanna. Well, Jake loved the stick and got on really well with my dad, who invited Jake and half the band to his house after the gig. This was the beginning of Regal Tip's long and close association and friendship with many of the greatest drummers in the world. It is well known that companies connect themselves with the "stars" in order to promote their products. Think Nike.

But we also associate with players because we rely on their input and ideas. After all, these are the people that are out there using the product. That night in the early '60s with the Woody Herman Band, Jake started talking about his ideas for his "perfect" stick. He was looking for a medium shaft stick with the new nylon tip, but with a slight back-end taper.

Jake was sent several designs until one suited him "perfectly." Jake's was the first name to ever go on a Regal Tip stick, our first Performer Series drumstick. We always knew where Jake's travels took him as we'd inevitably get orders from whatever part of the world he'd been to. Jake and my dad remained good friends and often stayed up until the middle of the night, talking "drums" and laughing a lot.

As I mentioned, Jake's was the first name that Regal Tip ever put on a stick and that had to have been around 1961. Our relationship with Jake spanned just about 50 years. My dad met him that night that he played with the Woody Herman band in Buffalo. A friendship developed that lasted until Jake's death, and there was a great deal of loyalty on both sides.

We used to bring Jake to the trade shows (NAMM[21] and PASIC) whenever he wanted to or was able to be there. Jake would hang until the early morning hours and show up at the booth generally around noon or 1 p.m. In the meantime, people would know that Jake would be at the show, and they'd keep coming to the booth to ask for him. This would go on all morning until he showed up. Jake was so personable and funny that people enjoyed hanging out with him. One year, before one of the NAMM shows, I made up some stickers that said, "Anyone seen Jake?" and passed them out at the show for people to wear, including Woody Herman who happened to be at this show. When Jake finally made his appearance sometime in the early afternoon, he kept running into people walking around with the "Jake" badges. He really enjoyed it.

For as much fun as we had together, Jake was there for us when we really needed him. Back in 1979 our factory was on strike, and my dad decided not to leave work to go to the NAMM show. Just my mother and I and one of our salespeople went. Jake was with us and when he found out that my dad and brother weren't going to come, he made sure to stay at the booth from the opening to the closing of the show, helping us out as much as he possibly could.

Carol Calato in Drumhead Magazine

I had the opportunity to play with Jake on Cape Cod and in Boston at Scullers Jazz Club. He was larger than life, a superb musician and a warm person to a young bass player.

Marshall Wood

My dad, Joe Conigliaro, grew up in Boston and used to play with Gene Krupa. That's where he first met Jake, sometime in the late `40s.

---

21   National Association of Music Merchants.

My first memory of Jake was him coming over one night when he and my parents were going to dinner and to hear Gene Krupa play. Jake was the odd man out because he had no date. He said something funny like he dropped her off along the way or that she got lost, and I thought what a trip he was. They all were wearing tuxedos, but he had an old raincoat over his — later it reminded me of Columbo's raincoat[22]. They were kidding him because he looked handsome in his tux but was wearing this ripped raincoat.

Years later when I was working in New York I would go to the China Song where the musicians hung out. Jake showed up when he was in town, and one night in `79 or `80 we ran into each other and happened to leave at the same time. He was getting into a cab and said, "Hey come along with me, I want you to meet some guys." We talked baseball until we got to this little joint downtown around Hudson Street, filled with a bunch of Woody Herman guys, Michael Moore on bass, Johnny Bunch on piano, Wayne Wright on guitar, Ruby Braff and Woody. Jake had me sit on the couch next to Astrud Gilberto! As a young songwriter I was utterly tongue-tied and just sat there for the session. It was around the time of the oil embargo, and they were doing a very funny version of the "Sheikh of Araby" with a real up tempo, as fast as they used to play "Caldonia," and they changed the words and sang, "The oil belongs to me." They played stop-time,[23] and Jake and Michael Moore just kept going.

It was so giving of Jake to invite me along for that memorable evening.

Brian Conigliaro

I'm a bass player, and I worked with Jake off and on for 35 years. He enjoyed working with me, and I felt honored as he was *very* picky about bass players. He recommended me for lots of work, which was invaluable in getting my career started, especially

------

22 Jake later became a great fan of Inspector Columbo.

23 Stop-time is when you interrupt, or stop, the normal time and alternate every other measure with silence or solos

during my early years in Los Angeles. If I told a bandleader that Jake said to call, that always got me the gig.

Paul Gormley

Before I met Jake, when I played with guys who knew him, especially Mike Moore, the conversations always got around to him. They'd say, "Jake would do it like this, or that." I really wanted to emulate him. I bought all the Woody Herman records I could find, and cut out Downbeat articles. He was such a phenomenal player; he had such great chops, a real innovator.

When I finally met him he showed me lots of stuff, I felt like he was "Doctor Hanna," answering my questions, telling me what I was doing wrong. He was so open and helpful, always had suggestions.. Some musicians get stuck up after they make it, but not him.

Joe Corsello

Jake was still on Woody's band when I first joined, though he left about three weeks later. But that brief time playing with him was a college education intensified into a quick cramming session. I had been listening to Jake play with Woody for years, but as any good musician will tell you, hearing someone and playing with them are not the same. Once you are on the bandstand, either as a jazz soloist or as a lead player, *that* is when you find out about what's deep inside the drummer's mind and body as far as the real swing pocket feel, at any tempo or style. Jake could hear and *feel* the eighth-note lines that were being played by the soloist and his body perfectly lined up with those lines to make everyone and everything swing so easily. He was not just a drummer, he was a musician, a true horn player on the inside. I did a fair amount of playing with him in L.A., but never enough.

I used to hang out at A.J. Kahn's home where Jake was residing. A.J. was a cousin of the great drummer, Tiny Kahn, but not a musician himself. He was one of the directors of the Los Angeles Institute of Social and Psychological Research. He was born in a small town in Georgia and had the accent to go with his roots. He had somehow lost an eye as a child and wore glasses with one lens opaque so his empty socket could not be seen. A.J. loved swing big bands mostly but revered all jazz music with a passion. His favorite was Bill Holman but also Nat Pierce, another Bostonian and long-time friend of Jake's.

Jake and A.J. together were a Laurel and Hardy-like act of comedic lines, constantly referencing one of their heroes, Lord Buckley (a fantastic American comedian-philosopher who was way ahead of his time and inspired Lenny Bruce, Steve Allen, and almost every other comedian who came after him).

Jake and A.J. always offered residence whenever my wife and I visited, and we enjoyed their social offerings and hospitality. I wish it all still existed today. These were valuable times in my early career, and I was blessed to have had both social and musical connections with Jake, certainly one of the truly *great* musicians and drummers!

Bobby Shew

Oh, I loved Jake. I met him years ago, even before I met Don. He was a big help and encouraged me in my singing. When Don and I got married, he and Jake developed a mutual admiration society. They loved and respected each other and their work. It was fun to be around them. Jake would ask Don about certain ways that he played, and then Don would do the same thing with him. They were real professionals, always learning. They never felt like they'd arrived, they kept working at it.

Jake was a unique guy, a loving human being and a great musician. I never heard him say an unkind word about anyone. He was never evil or bitter. Naturally there'd be some judgmental calls from time to time but even when he came out with one of his comments, it was always done truthfully, with a bit of humor. There was a unique and extraordinary kindness about him.

Terry Lamond

In December of 1983 I heard that Jake was accepting private students, primarily for brush playing on the snare drum and playing swing (jazz) on a ride cymbal/hi-hat. I called, introduced myself, told him who I was studying with at the time and said I wanted to learn how to play better swing time and brushes. I figured that playing better swing time on a cymbal would naturally transfer itself to the brushes. We set up a day and time.

Jake greeted me at the door when I arrived, and we carried on as if we'd known each other already, conversing for a good while before the lesson took place. Jake had set up a hi-hat stand with the hi-hat cymbals, snare in the middle and a cymbal stand with his famous ride cymbal (great sounding cymbal!). We sat down, and he began to explain along these lines:

"Now Vic, here's how this works. I figure if you can't play good swing time on a cymbal or hi-hat without the rest of the drums, then it won't make a bit of difference."

Then he said with seriousness and humor — I figured out the humor later — "I charge $30 an hour and 50¢ for every minute after that" (which would've been $30 had I stayed another hour).

He then asked me to play some swing time on the ride cymbal, liked what he heard and said, "Oh man, this is going to be a breeze, I'm not even going to charge you."

He made one slight adjustment, and I was okay after that. Along with the swing time on the cymbal, I still use that stuff we did with brushes to this day, and it has given me mileage over the years.

The best part of the lesson was that it ended up being three hours, or $90 according to Jake's math. But he didn't charge me at all. It was a wonderful and musical gift!

Vic Barrientos

It's almost impossible to describe the relationship of a bass player and drummer. When they play together, in order for it to be the best, your hearts have to be in sync, beating at the same time. You have to feel the beat, the 1 2 3, you have to feel that the same way.

If you set a metronome and tell people to count in sync with it, it will feel slightly different. For a drummer to play a ride cymbal pattern there was something about Jake's pulse, the rhythmic pulse he played with, like nobody else. There was something truly magical about it. It was absolutely effortless. When I played with him after not playing for a while, within two measures he'd look over at me, smile, and say, "Lu-u-u-thah, my man!" And we'd be right in sync.

Luther Hughes

I first heard Jake play at the Hickory House with the Toshiko Akiyoshi Trio when I was about 17. I played the bass so I was more interested in Gene Cherico who was so great. But I knew who Jake was. Then I heard him play with Maynard at Birdland and he really sparked up the whole band. A few years later I was working at a country club in Pennsylvania when the Woody Herman band came to play. After they performed some of the guys came into the bar where I was playing and they must have liked my playing because after a few tunes they asked if I'd like to play a jam session the next day with the band. Jake took my number after that and called me a few years later to play at the Half Note in New York with Bill Berry, Richie Kamuca and Nat Pierce.

I definitely credit Jake with helping me get my career started after I moved to LA in '68. He started calling me for various gigs, to play bass in Nat Pierce's big band, for another reunion with his NY guys, he got me on the Herb Ellis Quartet and we worked 3 or 4 years on and off at Donte's. He called me up to record for Concord. I think he liked me because I didn't have a big ego and wasn't pushy and didn't have an attitude. Plus he liked my playing.

Jake always seemed to be in good spirits and good health. He wanted to play jazz, and a certain kind of jazz, and that's what he did. I considered it a great privilege to play with him.

Herb Mickman

I had the honor of working with Jake over the last 20 or more years. I learned a lot from him, and it was always a joy to play with him. During the first set of every gig we worked, I would look over at him to see if the groove was good, and if he was smiling, I knew all was well. I think most the time he was smiling. Many of the jobs I've worked over the years were because Jake asked for me. Because of him I had the opportunity to work and record with many great musicians. I have always appreciated and will never forget how much he helped me.

Sometimes between tunes, Jake would have some funny remarks and kept us laughing. He liked to swing. When I worked with him, he did not care to play Latin tunes and always liked the bass to walk in four. I learned from Jake to keep the bass amp volume down, which I agree with.

There is one night that stands out in my memory. We were playing with Harry Allen in Half Moon Bay, and Jake was playing so-o-o great! It was a serious night of great jazz. Even though we had played many jobs before, the way Jake played this night was special. I will never forget it.

Dave Stone

I went to Jake's house one day with my brushes and got a three-hour master class.

I'd already been playing for years but wanted to "up my game," not only to get better with the brushes, but also to learn the little subtleties that you may not know in big band playing. So I went to the best. I already knew him but was still nervous about working with him.

First, I listened to him play. He showed me some rhythms and brush sweeps and certain ways to play brush time, brush beat, brush groove, sliding back and forth across the drum. Then we played trading fours and eights, the techniques of playing brushes. He also told me to listen to records and copy the sound. Sometimes you have to hear a master player tell you that. Now that I teach, I realize that while you might already know that, when a master tells you it makes a difference.

He taught me how to get the sound, the swish, and the sway with the brush, as well as the subtlety. It was a nice sound. I got so much out of it. That's why I called it a master class with Jake. It was an education, it was about learning from someone who's been there and done it.

Jack LeCompte

I was very excited about my first lesson with Jake. I really wanted to learn how he got that swinging groove on the brushes. Most drummers don't really play the brushes, but I wanted to learn how to play great with a subtle swish of sound that makes all the musicians on the bandstand really feel it. Jake was the way to achieving that goal. The first day we talked and worked on the snares. He had me start with a new stroke in each hand: left hand back and forth up the left side of the snare drum. The right hand had to lay flat and essentially do the standard ride cymbal jazz beat with a back and forth motion, right to left. The hand should hold the brush as flat as possible as opposed to a typical up and down motion with a wooden drumstick. Then he beat his hands on his chest with a shuffle beat: bum-ba-dum-ba-dum-ba-dum-ba-dum, over and over. He told me the secret to this technique for brushes was to get that shuffle feeling into it. It was not a straight-eights motion, but a shuffle beat. That's what made the sound really swing. I practiced it at home for three hours every day, and when I came back for my next lesson, Jake was happy I had done that. He said I was really starting to sound good. He had let many students go for not practicing what he taught them.

He took a lot of time for my lessons, though there was never any set period of time. Later he taught me how to do a ride cymbal beat that I had done for many years but never thought I needed lessons. But he told me to listen to Kenny Clarke groove away with his jazz beat on Miles Davis 1954 album, "Bag's Groove." I bought the CD and practically wore it out listening to the cymbal beat on that one tune.

Jake changed a lot of things in my drumming that year. I only paid $100 for the first lesson and $50 for the second one. After that, I brought him sushi for lunch, and he never charged me again. I brought him interesting CDs of drummers he had not heard before, brushes given to me from a manufacturer, and other things. But he always stuck to his old Cappella sticks (B.R.- Buddy Rich branded) and old Paiste 602 cymbal, which had a crystal clear sound that could never be repeated. We talked and talked about musicians, recordings, tunes, drums, everything, for hours at each lesson. He became more of a mentor and friend as the years went by. I visited him about six or seven times a year.

Joel Minamide

My lessons with Jake began with common-sense advice regarding how to set up the drums and how to set *myself* up at the drums: Sit with legs parallel to the floor; keep cymbals and drums close together. He said to use a follow-through stroke after touching the drums and cymbals with sticks and brushes, and used a sports analogy (follow-through swing with a baseball bat). He also told me to let the bass drum beater work *for* the drummer through use of gravity.

He asked me to play a ride cymbal beat. I did, with the second and fourth beat accented. Jake quickly said, "I didn't say "Play DIXIELAND"." He showed me a variation on the basic "ride" beat, which I use to this day.

Near the end of the lesson, he asked me to play brushes on the snare drum. I played a fast beat that I worked out myself, one I had not heard or seen other drummers play. Jake said, "Show me that again." I obliged. He said, "Let me try that." He did. Then he said, "Ahhh. I'll use that the next time I play with Teddy Wilson!"

My brush beat: "Show me that again. Ahh. I'll use that the next time I play with Teddy Wilson."

The lessons were daunting because I had so much to work on, but also exhilarating. How many drummers were fortunate enough to take lessons from a master swinger like Jake Hanna?

Hal Smith

I have always been a fan of Jake Hanna's drumming, and was lucky to spend some quality time with him during a session in Ireland at the Guinness Cork Jazz Festival. We both sat in with a group playing in the hotel bar, and Jake was incredibly supportive and complementary. He really was taken with the way I used my right hand on the cymbal. I explained that it was the method taught by my teacher, Joe Morello. I in turn complemented him on his playing, and his important influence on all drummers.

I had been mainly a fan of Jake's playing from his recordings with Woody Herman, but I recently found out that he was the drummer on one of my favorite recordings. My 2011 workbook, "The Evolution of Jazz Drumming," featured Jake along with 30 other jazz drumming greats. In the text I mentioned that one of my favorite recordings was Maynard Ferguson's "Message from Newport." I always thought that the drummer on that recording was Rufus "Speedy" Jones, and that is how I listed the information in the text. After the book was published, I received an e-mail from a knowledgeable drummer, who wrote that he thought it was Jake, not Speedy. I looked it up, and sure enough, he was the magical drummer I'd been listening to all these years! The recording is a classic, and Jake's playing just stellar. In honor of his innovative playing, here is a brief commentary on the 6 tracks of that recording:

Maynard's Message from Newport, starts with a medium up tempo swinger, "Fan It, Janet." The tune showcases Jake's ride beat, and his triplet based fills. His snare sound is fantastic, and he plays some great cross stick fills at the end of the tune. It is followed by "The Waltz," which features Jake's great time playing in three. The swinging feel is right down the middle, and his use of the bass drum on downbeats anchors the time without making it feel stiff.

Next up is another medium up swing tune, "And We Listened." Jake plays some nice be-bop fills using stick on stick accents. You can also really hear the beautiful ring of his ride cymbal, as well as his solid beat behind all the trombone and sax solos. His time is fantastic. About 4 minutes into the tune, you can hear him use those rim shots to accentuate horn figures during a crescendo section, and nice little bass drum fills at the end. "Tag Team" is a slower swing tune that starts by showcasing Jake's swinging brush time feel. His great fills and behind the beat execution of the figures makes this a wonderfully musical track. He then switches to sticks and here's his great swinging "down the middle" ride beat providing a cushion for the entire band. I love his fills and sets ups in the last part of the song, allowing for powerful dynamics without sacrificing the time feel.

The next track, "Slide's Derangement," is one of the greatest big band drumming performances of all time. Jake's swinging time feel, use of fills, dynamics, cross stick accents, and ride cymbal sound are a joy. His solos at the end of the tune are melodic, energy providing, and inspirational. The recording sounds as fresh today as when it was recorded in 1958. The following tune, "Frame for the Blues," is another amazing example of Jake's melodic, sensitive and swinging drumming. It's a classic slow blues, and his time feel and fills are incredible. The out chorus is a brilliant display of dynamics from powerful fills back down to brushes for the last melody. "Three Little Foxes" ends the album with a fast burning Maynard swinger. Jake's time feel, ride cymbal, and fills drive the band.

I recommend this — and really any of Jake's recordings — to all serious students of the drums. His playing, and his role as an innovative and creative drummer, is an integral part of jazz drumming history. Thanks, Jake for your incredible playing and timeless musical inspiration!

Danny Gottlieb

"Kid, you're doing good."

I never expected to hear something like that from Jake, to have him to tell me he liked where I was going musically. Now Jake liked music and he liked lyrics—he knew the lyrics to so many songs — but so many singers didn't sing jazz the way he thought it should be sung. And when they didn't, he wasn't polite. So the fact that he stayed through a whole set where I was singing ... wow!

I was around him for 16 years at jazz festivals and at his house, but I felt like I grew taller because of that comment. It was about six months before he died.

Ava DuPree

[Advice for percussionists] I would recommend listening to CDs of the great drummers, Krupa and Rich, Dave Tough for cymbals, Denzel Best for brushes and Jo Jones for anything. Also get film of them and watch them play. Don't try to copy any one of them. Just practice religiously and what you heard and saw will kick in and you'll come up with your own style. I feel very fortunate that when I was starting out I was able to see and hear in person all those famous drummers at the RKO in Boston. That's how I learned. Those big band days with all the many outstanding drummers were a unique period of time that we'll probably never see again.

Jake Hanna as told to John Tumpak

Who's Getting Whose Drums?

Joe Ascione

I wish I carried a tape recorder as I walked around with Jake during the 25 years I knew him. He had an uncanny ability to reference names, places, dates, specifics, like no one else.

I loved how, when asked about a certain person—Gene Krupa for instance—he'd rattle off times and places and encounters they had in New York and Boston, how they'd get off an all-night gig, have breakfast, they even went to Mass together.

Growing up I had all the drum magazines and read stories about my heroes—Gene Krupa, Sonny Payne, Jo Jones, Louis Bellson, Jake Hanna, Buddy Rich and Ed Shaughnessy. So when I got a call 25 years ago to play the West Texas Jazz Party and found out Jake was going to be the other drummer, I was ecstatic. It seemed to me that Jake either liked you—and you may not have known it—or he didn't like you and you knew it.

When I first met him it was exciting to find out he appreciated what I was doing on the instrument. We were talking in the green room and the hospitality suite one night after we finished playing, and I started picking his brain. I thought to myself, *I'm gonna try to keep up with this guy*, but before I knew it the sun was coming up, and I looked at my watch, and it was after 7 in the morning. I tried to leave, but Jake said, "Joe, you're not goin' anywhere, have another beer."

I was fortunate to share the stage with him at many jazz parties and talk to him. I could ask him about anyone, about Bing, and Rosie, or Joe Louis or baseball players. He had stories about them all.

I can tell my students about Jake, but they'll never experience him first hand, or sit down at a table with him and witness him first hand. When I used to set up Buddy Rich's drums I had that experience.

He definitely helped me in my career. If Jake Hanna says positive things about your musicianship, everyone else views you with a certain amount of respect. Jake would tell the musicians, "Joe Ascione, he's the best. No one else can do it." That's the ticket.

When I was a kid, Louis Bellson told me, "Always play with people who are better than you. And when you send subs, send good subs because that makes you look good." I can't tell you how many times the phone would ring and someone would say Jake gave us your number. He told Roberta Gambarini about me, and I got to work with her at the Nairn Jazz Festival in Scotland. He was instrumental—pardon the pun—by giving me a positive stamp, his blessing, because others respected his opinion.

He was always quick with words, but a man of few words when it came to certain things.

Every festival, when I saw him setting up his cymbals, he'd say to me, "Joe, these are yours." Then he'd add, "But not yet, Joe, not yet," putting up his hands to fend me off. He meant, of course, that one day he was going to leave me his cymbals.

The first time I saw him after I had been diagnosed with Multiple Sclerosis, I noticed he was a little quiet. Then he looked up at me and said, "Joe, I may be getting *yours*."

I said, "Jake, you son of a bitch."

That was priceless.

As a drummer, fan and friend, I think of him every day and miss him a lot. And I've got his hi-hats. Denisa came up to me at the San Diego Jazz Party, and I saw she had them in her hands. We both had tears in our eyes as she handed them to me.

INTERLUDE

Yeah Johnny Boy

John Allred

Jake was such a huge supporter of me and my career. He went out of his way to tell people about me and to check me out when I was trying to make some sort of name for myself.

Back in 1995 when I was dating a Swiss girl and hanging out in Bern, Switzerland, for months at a time, I would go into Marian's Jazz Room to see the guys play. Jake was there one week playing with Ralph Sutton, another hero of mine. Ralph and Jake saw me come in and waved me up to the stand before they were even finished with their first set. I was excited to feel so welcomed into their fold that night. I ended up playing the rest of their set and most of the next set as well. I was on Cloud Nine. Fortunately for me, the club owner, Hans Zurbrugg, was in the room that evening with his wife Marian, the namesake of the club, and they got to hear me play. On the break between sets, Ralph and Jake both strongly suggested that Hans hire me sometime to play in his club. Within a year Hans called me with an invitation to bring my own band over to the club to do a week.

During the next few years Jake and Ralph dropped my name everywhere they could. I played with them both a handful of times in Denver at the Park Hill Golf Resort, and also in Odessa, Tex; San Diego; Kingsport, Tenn; several more times in Bern; Elkhart, Ind; Sarasota, Fla; Aspen, Col; and at Sunny Sutton's Rocky Mountain Jazz Party in Denver for at least six years.

The first recording of Jake I had was an LP on Concord called the "Hanna-Fontana Band Live at the Pavilion." Carl Fontana had been one of my musical heroes for years, and he and Jake were very close. I played that record over and over and over again until the needle wouldn't even stay in the groove. I couldn't bear to throw it out, so I followed the advice I'd gotten somewhere to take an old LP and lay it on top of a round bowl and place it in an oven and heat it up. The end result was a perfectly shaped bowl! I put a piece of tape over the hole in the record and used it to serve chips at parties. It was coveted by my trombone friends for years.

Finally one day I ran across a CD reissue of the LP and bought it. It should last me a while. I think that Jake could hear a little bit of Fontana's style in my playing and liked that.

The best nine weeks of my life were those spent with a small band that Warren Vaché put together to tour the states with a swing dance troupe from the UK in a show called "Swingtime." Warren was also someone who influenced me greatly, and he had Randy Reinhart, Chuck Wilson, Harry Allen, Ricky Woodard, Steve Ash, Murray Wall and Jake. We did one nighters all across the country and had a blast.

This trip was very special to me since Jake and I had both done road time with the great Woody Herman Big Band, years apart, but we still had the Woody Herman connection. So to get a chance to actually ride the same band bus with Jake was an honor in itself. We had millions of laughs along the way. I cracked Jake up numerous times with my "Bubba Teeth," plastic joke teeth that you could form fit over your real teeth but they looked like the worst hillbilly rotten teeth you'd ever seen. Since we were on the road for Columbia Artists, once in a while the band would be asked to attend a sponsor party after the show. We didn't always feel like participating, so one evening when Warren came down the bus aisle to announce that we had to make another after party, a couple of us put in the fake teeth and made our best attempt at a backwoods redneck accent as we asked, "Izzit Mandan-torry?" Jake just about hit the floor. We got out of having to make those sponsor parties after that!

Once we saw how much Jake liked them, we would stick in the teeth and go into a little hillbilly act just to get a rise out of him. Every time I saw Jake after that tour he would try to imitate our hillbilly act and stick his teeth out and laugh. He had the greatest sense of humor and was so much fun to sit around and laugh with.

Towards the end of that tour, Warren decided to rent a jeep and drive around the area. He took off that morning on our day off and returned early that afternoon to report that he spent $150 on a rental car only to find out there was nothing within driving distance. So three of us guys hopped into the jeep, and Warren decided that doing some four-wheeling on the hotel property would be fun. We bounced around the lot for a while before we noticed Jake standing beside the hotel looking straight up at the sky. Warren quietly pulled the jeep up right next to Jake and startled him saying "Hey Jakey, what the hell are you doing?" Without missing a beat Jake looks at us all and says, "I'm staring at the sun like a fuckin' mystic." We all completely lost it, and that quote echoed in the bus for the rest of the trip.

Jake was quite good at picking just the right second to make a funny statement. In Sacramento one year a bunch of us guys were hanging out at the bar in the back of the Martinique Room at the Red Lion Inn where the all-star bands played. Jake walks in, and listened to a few choruses of the band playing—now granted, they were having a hard time keeping the tempo from dragging as they were playing a slow number—and it was getting slower by the second. "Well," Jake says, seemingly just as the room went quiet, "20 bucks say they stop before the end of the next chorus." The cats at the bar were on the floor. Jake was a no-bullshit guy and called things just as he saw them. I loved that about him.

There's no way to describe how great I felt during my solos when I heard Jake say, "Yeah Johnny Boy." I knew just in that moment that I must have done something right.

I can't tell you how many times and how many people that I have told that Jake was my absolute favorite person in the world. I would have done anything for that man, and there is no way possible to measure the amount of respect that I have for him, his music and his attitude toward life. I love him dearly and will miss him every day for the rest of my life.

CHAPTER

12

Jake and Denisa

There were several bachelor uncles in the Hanna and Nichols family. Jake's older brother Billy never married.

Family and friends assumed Jake would become another bachelor uncle. Then he met Denisa.

Denisa Heitman grew up in a small town outside Colorado Springs where she began playing piano at age two. She switched to the guitar when she was 12 and started giving lessons a few months later. She began playing professionally while she was still in high school, which is when she met the great guitarist Johnny Smith. He took her under his wing and taught her jazz guitar and guitar repair. She played the French horn, guitar and upright bass at the University of Colorado and played bass and guitar for the Colorado Springs Symphony. She was working for Johnny in 1978 when a swinging drummer came to town.

Jake liked to come to Colorado after we finished with Bing's tour. Denisa was working at the music store my wife and I owned. That's where they met and that was the beginning of the love story.

Jake handled everything lightly, so he didn't stop with the one-liners after he got married.

Johnny Smith

We first saw Jake and Denisa together at the Odessa, Texas Jazz Party. They were sitting on the far side of the pool, away from the group that was having fun and drinking. Someone would ask who that young girl was with Jake, and the joke was "Oh, that's his niece, Denisa."

When we saw him after that we'd ask about his niece.

Dale and Nancy Hibler

It was always great to be with Jake and Denisa. At first we were surprised he married someone so young, but she fit right in.

Sunny Sutton

Jake took our brother, Billy, on a cruise in 1975. This was the one where he paid him back for co-signing the loan for his drums back in 1949. Billy used to get up early to walk around the deck, and one morning he began chatting with a tall, imposing looking man who was also a regular walker.

"Did you hear the band last night?" the fellow asked. "Boy, I thought that drummer was great. I'd certainly like to meet him some time."

"Well you won't meet him at this time of day because he doesn't get up much before noon," Bill advised. "And I should know because I'm his brother."

The fellow never did meet Jake on that cruise, but during their morning walks he and Billy exchanged information and it turned out that he lived in the same town we did. I met him shortly after the cruise, and we became good friends. Bob was a retired FBI agent who was the Chief of Police at Harvard University, and he was a huge jazz fan. (In fact, he was so knowledgeable about music that Harvard assigned him to be freshman advisor to a number of students who were in the band. You can imagine how they felt upon discovering their advisor was the Chief of Police).

Jake came to Boston for a visit in 1982, and our sister Mary organized a dinner. We thought it would be nice to invite Bob so he could finally meet Jake. The two of them hit it off and spent most of the evening sitting together talking about jazz. They kept up a correspondence, and that was how we discovered Jake and Denisa were getting married.

In the fall of 1984 Bob got a postcard from Jake that read: "In Russia with Fraser McPherson. Denisa and I getting married when I get back."

Bob called to tell me, and I called my sister Mary.

"Did you know Jake was getting married?" I asked her.

She hadn't gotten a postcard either.

Eleanor Hanna Judge

My father [Joe Calato] told me this story. It's one of his favorites.

My parents were invited to Jake and Denisa's wedding, something they would never miss! My father couldn't believe that Jake was finally getting married. So they made a trip out of it and drove across country from New York to California. They hung out with friends for a couple of days, and then it was the wedding day. Everyone showed up at the home at which they were getting married.

It just so happened that the baseball playoffs were being held on that same day and the Red Sox were in the playoffs. So, first things first. The actual ceremony kept being delayed until the end of the game. Jake had his priorities! I'm sure Denisa knew Jake well enough by then not to be surprised.

Carol Calato

Jake and Denisa gave us a hard time about not attending their wedding. We told them we waved as we went by. They said, "You mean you were driving by and you just waved?"

"No, we were flying overhead on our way to a jazz party in the Bay Area."

Dale and Nancy Hibler

I started at UCLA in the fall of 1984 and went to Jake and Denisa's wedding a few weeks later. I saw them often that first year although later our schedules kept us pretty busy. I'd house-sit for them when they went away, and sometimes we'd go to Donte's. I was very impressed that the bartender was Lee Ving from the band Fear, a far cry from the world of jazz. Jake and Denisa were always so nice to me and such fun to be around.

Paula Judge

When Jake came to our Air Force Band reunion in 1984, we were thrilled to meet Denisa. They seemed so well suited and so happy together.

Richard Boubelik

Jake sent shock waves through the Concord offices when he announced he was getting married. We couldn't believe after all these years he was marrying someone so much younger. Carl Jefferson gave it a month, and he wasn't the only one. But Denisa's personality totally dove-tailed with Jake's, and she was perhaps the best thing that ever happened to him. She made him happy and theirs was a marriage to be envied to the very end.

I have a fond memory of sitting in Jake and Denisa's "bar room," the walls papered with U.S. currency, autographed dollar bills for the most part. My friend, Margy Coate, and I signed our names to a five-dollar bill and it was added to the collection.

The world is full of odd coincidences. It turns out my son-in-law was close to Jake's sister Eleanor and her family in Hull, MA (and a high school classmate of the author of this book). I was delighted to meet them, and when Eleanor came to San Francisco to visit offspring, we all got together.

I remember telling her that I was surprised to find that Jake had a family, I'd always felt he was hatched from an egg. He was definitely one of a kind.

Merrilee Trost

I went to see Jake in the '90s when I felt I was at a turning point in my life, and I said "Uncle Jake, I'm thinking of getting married." A look came over his face that I'd never seen before and he grabbed me by the shoulders with both hands and said, "Jackson, why? I got married when I was 54 and I should have waited."

Denisa was standing nearby and she clunked our heads together like Moe did to Curly and Larry.

Jake didn't follow his own advice of course, and I know why. He had met and married a wonderful woman.

Jack Howard

Jake and Denisa were such a good fit. I had a music business for more than 20 years, so I knew about him long before he became my son-in-law. Jake really loved family and had such a soft heart. I used to ask him about famous people in the music industry — he seemed to know them all — and if he liked them he would say, "Great guy, great guy," with the word "guy" dragged out, as only he could say it. And Rosemary Clooney was a "Great ga-a-a-l... great singer."

I spent a month with them when Denisa was in the hospital and Jake and I got along famously. I walked to and from the hospital every day, and Denisa and I played cards when she felt up to it.

My watch started to lose time while I was there, and Jake told me about a place he'd seen on his own walks where I might get a "good deal." We walked so far that by the time we arrived at what

I think was a pawn shop, I was totally lost. We had a great time and found a watch for $25. I barely got my money's worth out of it because it quit on me after I returned home. I mentioned it to Denisa, and shortly after that Jake returned from a trip to Sweden or Germany with a lovely watch for me. I still wear it with a smile on my face.

I have so many wonderful, touching memories of Jake and his kindness and tender heart.

Pat Domroese

We first met Jake and Denisa at a Jazz party in Victoria, B.C. Jake and my husband, Bill, hit it off, and after that we saw them often. We'd get together at jazz parties and festivals, they'd come to our apartment in Vancouver and to our home in a logging camp on northern Vancouver Island. We also stayed with them in their home and traveled to jazz festivals together.

I can picture him and hear his voice as he was in raconteur mode in the late — sometimes very late — evenings when everyone was having a great time. They're very fond memories.

Jan Moore

Jake and Denisa came on our honeymoon with us. We got married in Sacramento at the end of August and then drove down to L.A. to the Jazz Festival. After that the four of us went to Catalina Island and that became an annual event for many years. Denisa and Howard would go swimming or surfing while Jake and I hung out in the bar, or sunned ourselves. One day the four of us were sitting on the beach reading. Jake had James Michener's *Hawaii*, Denisa was reading a detective story, I was reading *Scarlett* and Howard was reading *All Quiet on the Western Front*. People walking by would give us these strange looks. One guy stopped, stared at us, and finally said, "What's wrong with this picture?"

Terrie Richards

Bill and I spent a lot of time with Jake and Denisa. We all lived in L.A. and had the same friends. I knew Jake for more than 50 years. I met him back in Cincinnati—I think that was before Bill and I got married. Jake was Bill's favorite drummer and he hired him every time he could. They went back to Woody Herman days and also worked together on the Merv Griffin Show. I produced the International Jazz party that Bill and Eiji Kitamura founded and Jake played with them.

They were so much fun to be with. Denisa did a lot of entertaining and we went to their house for parties and for Christmas dinner.

I adored them. I miss Jake.

Betty Berry

We spent a lot of time with Jake and Denisa because we were always at the same jazz parties. I loved them. I think Denisa is amazing. Intellectually they were beautifully matched, with similar senses of humor and a shared love of music. She always took care of him, always knew what was going on.

Elsa Davern

I used to house for Jake and Denisa and watch the cats when they went away. They flew to New York City on September 10, 2001 for a recording date and of course they couldn't fly home until they reopened the airports. So I stayed there with the cats for a whole week.

Polly Podewell

Denisa took very good care of Jake. And she was so resourceful. Jake was out of town during the Northridge earthquake, and she drained the water heater. Everyone else wound up with rusted out water heaters, but she knew enough to drain theirs.

Eleanor Hanna Judge

Denisa made lasagna the second time Charlie Watts and Jim Keltner came to dinner. It was delicious, all the more so because the oven went on the fritz and wouldn't heat up higher than a mild sweat. You could touch the pan with your finger and it didn't hurt. Denisa and I were laughing about what we could serve the guests if the main course came out of the oven as cold as it went in.

Rory and I had come to L.A. to spend Thanksgiving with Jake and Denisa so we were fortunate to be there for the second "Dinner with Jake." Their home was a wonderful place to visit. Jake and Denisa had a way of welcoming you, of making you feel that your comfort was the most important thing to them. They were easy to be with, and so much fun. When you sleep over at someone's house and it's comfortable like that, you see your hosts in some new ways, quiet, more personal.

Jake had an economy in his movements around the house, a naturalness I found relaxing. He moved with purpose but didn't seem rushed. He took a broom and swept the sidewalks clean of the tree fallings. Such a little thing — I am not sure why it seems so important to me now. Maybe it reminded me of my own mother, of good citizenship. Jake was larger than life but he swept his own sidewalks.

I was nervous before dinner, Rory was filled with adrenaline, Denisa was cheerful and busy, and Jake was casual. Then Charlie and Jim arrived and Jake went off like a party popper on New Year's Eve; he was a supernova of fun and cheer. He was full of compliments and even his teasing felt like the highest praise. Jake knew about everything and had the goods on everybody. He had us all in a state of moderately controlled hysteria. Funny? Oh, man, our collective sides were aching. Forkfuls of lasagna, good red wine, crusts of bread, cheese, butter, stories, arms criss-crossing the small table like pickup sticks, laughter, tomato sauce spills on the table cloth ... that's how I remember dinner.

Scott Thorburn

I got married in Rosemary Clooney's back yard and Jake and Denisa came to our wedding. It was extraordinary to have them there. I respected Jake so much for his talent, advice and sense of humor.

Allen Sviridoff

I dropped in on Uncle Jake one year when I was in Los Angeles with some friends. It was an unexpected trip that we'd arranged quickly after one of the guys found a $99 round-trip fare advertised in the newspaper and called me at midnight from the airport to ask if I'd like to go along. (It turned out to be a misprint, but the airline had to honor the price).

I didn't think to get in touch with Jake and Denisa ahead of time, but I called them from Anaheim to say hello. Denisa invited me to spend the night, drove down to pick me up, and then took me around Los Angeles. She was very gracious and hospitable, but Jake seemed kind of annoyed that his routine had been disrupted. He didn't say anything, but I had the feeling he really wanted to just sit there reading his paper and wondered why I hadn't given him a month's notice before I dropped in.

Denisa was driving me back to my hotel the next day and as I was packing up to leave, I called out, "Jake, I'm going, thanks a lot," and he called back from the living room, "Okay, see you later." Denisa said, "Excuse me," stormed out of the room, and returned a minute later with Jake shuffling along behind her saying, "Oh, great to see you, great to see you." I'm sure she gave him hell and told him to get in there and say goodbye properly to your nephew.

Joe Howard

Life with Jake

Denisa Hanna

I met Jake when I was working for Johnny Smith.

It was the summer of 1978, and Johnny was worried about him. Jake had suffered three major losses in the previous two years. His housemate, A.J. Kahn, who he had lived with for six years, died in 1976. Then Bing Crosby died in September 1977, just days after Jake had finished touring with him. And his older brother, Billy, who he adored, had died suddenly, just a few weeks before we met.

Johnny was Bing's guitarist and got to know Jake when they played together on tour. They had lots of fun on the road, and Jake would periodically stop by Colorado Springs to visit Johnny. He arrived that June, and Johnny could see that he was depressed. He told me he'd take care of my guitar students that afternoon if I would take Jake around and keep him company. So I drove him to Canyon City in my Datsun 510, and we visited my parents at their music store where he signed a drum head. We talked about music during our drive, and I thought he was a nice guy, very funny, but no bells or whistles went off. On the way to the Royal Gorge we stopped at a farm stand famous for its fruit trees. We bought apple cider and cherry cider, and Jake drank about four bottles of them during the cocktail hour, instead of his customary martini. It turned out he had just gone on the wagon. That may have been another reason Johnny was worried.

He came out a few more times to see Johnny and then to see me, and we had a funny routine about olives. Johnny and the guys used to drink martinis, but not me since I hated gin. I did love olives, though, so the fellows always gave me the olives from their drinks. Jake didn't know this, of course, so he ate his olive (by this time he had resumed drinking), and Johnny said, "Why didn't you give that to Denisa?" Once the ritual was explained to him, he started giving me his olives. That routine continued for years. People would ask about it, and we explained how it started.

The following January I met him again at the NAMM Show, and then the bells and whistles did go off. Our first official date was at the West Texas Jazz Party in Odessa where we apparently were the talk of the town.

It was a romance that percolated slowly over several years. He took me on the road a few times, including a trip to Bern, Switzerland, with Ralph Sutton. That's when I discovered one of his bachelor routines involved soaking himself *and* his socks in the bathtub, together. I told him that was going to stop. My luggage got lost on the trip back to L.A. so he took me to the May Company to replenish the basics. I could tell he was embarrassed to be shopping for my underwear, but I could hardly go around without any. Later he took me on a cruise to the Hawaiian Islands, where I finally got my first look at the ocean.

Things were hectic, and I was spending lots of time in L.A. and not paying attention to my work with Johnny and then I found out that he had fired me. I'd known him for about 10 years at that point. Johnny and his wife were lovely people. They taught me how to eat, how to drink, and how to play, much like Woody did with Jake. I was pretty upset and called Jake in tears. Cal Collins was with him—they were working on a record—and they burst out laughing. I'm sure they didn't mean to sound heartless, but I did wonder what I was getting myself into. But I took the plunge and moved to L.A. to take up residence with Jake ... and Bernie.

Bernie had been Terry Gibbs' band boy and hung out at the house, probably part of the collection of occasional guests that A.J. had acquired over the years. After A.J. died, Bernie somehow wound up moving in with Jake, and by the time I arrived on the scene, he was pretty comfortably ensconced. So I had two roommates for a couple of years. Jake and I traveled a lot, and it was helpful to have Bernie there to handle phone calls and take messages about gigs ... or so we thought. Finally Jake realized that he wasn't getting the messages, so he asked Bernie to leave.

My mother and my sister both got married in 1984, and Jake must have decided a third celebration was in order, because he asked me to marry him.

It was a whirlwind year. He went off to Russia with Fraser McPherson, and I stayed in L.A. making plans for the wedding. He wrote me lots of letters on that trip—he usually wasn't much of a correspondent—but they didn't arrive until about two years later. I never got a letter from him after that.

Most people didn't know how old Jake was—he always looked younger than his years—so they weren't really aware of the 24 year age difference. But hopefully they noticed an improvement in his look once I came along because I purged his closets of a lot ugly clothes, especially his plaid collection.

Jake was very busy at that time. He had at least one job a month and traveled at lot. We spent about half the time on the road, because he worked more overseas and *on* the sea—he did lots of cruises when we first got married. We went to Germany with Peter Ralph, to London with Scotty Hamilton and Ruby Braff, around Holland and Germany with Woody's small band, to Switzerland, Ireland, Scotland and Norway. I never went on the trips to Japan, but I sure logged many miles.

Some of the miles were on foot. Jake was a great walker. I suppose he got in the habit when he was young because his family never had a car. At home he'd walk up to the Farmers Market and then keep going. He could spend all day out walking. It wasn't any kind of aerobic activity since he was rather pokey—they called him "The Snail" when he was in the Air Force—but he sure did like to meander.

I had a great life with Jake. He was extremely supportive of anything I did, and life was always interesting. We had similar senses of humor. I knew exactly what he was going to say when he started to say it. He was a very nice man, temperamental as musicians can be, but honest and loyal and true.

I think he would like to be remembered as a swinging drummer, not necessarily a great drummer, but one with integrity. He didn't go with the flow, but he knew exactly what he wanted to do, and he did it. He didn't die a rich man, but he died a happy man. Music was his life, and he was able to live it the way he wanted. Other drummers should listen to him.

He sure swung. He sure enjoyed it. He swung it *his way*.

C H A P T E R

13

You're *Jake Hanna's* sister/ niece . . . ?

Jake's family and childhood friends were sometimes surprised by reactions they got to the mention of his name. He certainly was well known in jazz circles and in drumming circles, but his relatives didn't travel in those circles, and he wasn't a household name. Nevertheless, family members delighted in exchanging stories about the different times Jake's name had come up in a conversation and led to a fascinating discussion with someone who turned out to be a huge fan.

The stories in this section come from family members and one fan.

One of my friends was taking a music-appreciation course through the Lifelong Learning Program at Boston College. She told me that one of the sessions was going to be about the Big Band Era and suggested I come to class with her that day. We brought a lunch and wound up sitting at the same cafeteria table as the teacher. My friend introduced me to him.

"This is my friend Mary Howard," she announced. "Her brother is a famous drummer."

"Oh," he said, politely, clearly not expecting much. "What's his name?"

I told him. He immediately moved over to sit next to us and began talking about Jake. He obviously was a big fan because he knew a lot about him and spoke quite knowledgeably.

When the class began, he made an announcement.

"We have a celebrity in class today, Jake Hanna's sister, Mary Howard."

I got a round of applause.

Mary Hanna Howard

I was moving out of my apartment in Boston's North End and hired a couple of fellows whose flyer I saw posted on a nearby telephone pole. After loading the truck, we were driving to my new home and got to chatting. They mentioned they were musicians studying at Berklee. One of them was a drummer.

"My uncle studied drumming at Berklee," I told them.

"Oh," they said, more out of politeness than interest. "What does he do now?"

"He's the drummer on "The Merv Griffin Show.""

The driver turned to stare at me in awe.

"Your uncle is *Jake Hanna*?"

My new best friends and I talked all the way home.

Maria Judge

I got friendly with a drum teacher at the place where I took guitar lessons. During one of our occasional jam sessions we started talking about drummers. I asked him if he knew much about jazz. He did, so I asked him if he'd ever heard of Jake Hanna. He had, which surprised me a bit because he was about my age, maybe even younger.

"He's my uncle," I told him.

"Really?" he said. He seemed taken aback.

"Yeah."

"Really?" he said again, then sat back in his chair, shaking his head in amazement.

He was quite impressed.

Joe Howard

I used to take communion to an elderly woman in town, and her son was often visiting her when I arrived. One day I told him that I wouldn't be able to come the following week, because I would be in California. He asked about the trip, and I told him my family was getting together at a jazz festival where my brother was playing. He asked who my brother was and I said, "Jake Hanna." "Never heard of him," he said.

When I got back from California I brought communion to her again. Her son answered the door and said, "I owe you an apology."

"Why," I asked.

"I Googled Jake Hanna," he told me.

Mary Hanna Howard

When I was in high school the band always played at the Christmas concert, and the alumni were invited back to perform. During my freshman year some older drummers came back to play, and after the concert I hitched a ride home with several of them. One guy said, "I heard there's a kid in the band whose uncle is Jake Hanna." Someone else said, "You're kidding." "He's *my* uncle!" I piped up from the back seat.

So instead of dropping me off at home, they took me out drinking and wanted to know all about Jake. I filled them in on what little I knew at the time, and without letting the truth get in the way of a good story, proceeded to BS my way through the rest of the evening.

Rory Judge

A colleague at MIT called with a question one afternoon in May 2002 and after we finished our business, we chatted for a while. I mentioned I was going to California over the Memorial Day weekend and she wondered if I was doing something fun. I told her we were going to the Sacramento Jazz Festival, adding that my uncle was the "Emperor"[24] that year.

She asked his name, and I told her. There was a pause, I heard her put the phone down, and less than a minute later she was standing in my doorway.

"You're Jake Hanna's niece?" she asked breathlessly. Turns out she was taught jazz piano and was a great fan.

I bought her back a festival T-shirt and a copy of the program that Jake had signed, "Keep swingin,' Barbara." She was thrilled.

"I told all my friends I work with Jake Hanna's niece," she informed me.

Maria Judge

I used to work for FEMA (Federal Emergency Management Agency) and went around the country to work on disasters. One year I was sent to Atlantic City and ran into a man named Bill Smith who was from the Denver office. Mark, a young man in our office, worked closely with him. One day he told me Bill was a big jazz fan and had taken him to a few clubs in New York City. I told Mark my brother was a jazz drummer.

Mark came into my office one day to say Bill Smith was on the phone and would like to talk to me. I got on the phone and Bill said, "I hear your brother is a jazz musician. I wanted you to know that I'm listening to some Concord Jazz right now. My friends and I tape their music whenever we hear it and pass it around."

"Who's the drummer on the recording?" I asked him.

"Jake Hanna."

"That's my brother," I told him.

---

24 An Emperor was chosen each year to be honored for his excellence and commitment to jazz.

Bill sure heard of *him*. Eventually he met Jake at some of the jazz parties he attended and sent me some pictures he took.

Eleanor Hanna Judge

My colleague Charlene was showing me some pictures from a family wedding. I noticed someone playing the drums in one of the pictures and asked who it was. She told me it was her brother Clayton, who had been a professional drummer. I said "My brother is a professional drummer." She asked his name and I told her.

Charlene had lunch almost every day with Clay, and she must have mentioned Jake to him the next day, because that afternoon my office door flew open, and there stood her brother.

"You're Jake Hanna's sister?"

From that point on he brought me all kinds of Jake memorabilia whenever he came across it.

Mary Hanna Howard

I'd been a fan of Jake Hanna's since 1965 when I first heard him play on my Woody Herman records. So I couldn't believe that *my* sister Charlene actually worked with *his* sister Mary.

Clayton White

My father and I were coming home from Cape Cod on the train, and Dad was being his usual loud, boisterous self. There were two couples nearby who were also talking up a storm, and it turned out they grew up in Dorchester, just like he did. Pretty soon they were trying to outdo each other with their Dorchester pedigrees.

One of the men said, "Oh, I lived on such and such a street, and one of the guys I hung around with was Jake Hanna."

My father said, "Oh, he's *my* brother-in-law."

The guy tosses out Jake's name to get some street cred, and it turns out he's talking to one of his relatives.

It was funny to have someone else drop his name for a change.

Joe Howard

Go East Young Man

Howard Alden

When I began playing the guitar I heard the first Concord Jazz recording with Joe Pass and Herb Ellis. I was interested in them because they were guitar players, but then I noticed Ray Brown and Jake Hanna were also on that record. I'd heard of Ray but not of Jake, and though I bought it mainly for the guitar players, I really liked his sound. Then I saw his name on a lot of other CJ records and was thrilled that such mainstream jazz was being recorded. I was introduced to him a few years later, and he said, 'You sound great, I love what you're doing, love that Charlie Christian stuff, great sound, great swing."

Shortly after Denisa moved to town, Jake asked if I'd give her lessons on the electric bass. I said okay, and he asked what I charged. "I guess $30," I told him. "I'll pay you $50," he said. So I'd go over to the house, show her some stuff I knew about basses and bass lines, they'd serve me dinner, then we'd sit around for another five hours talking, drinking and listening to music. We became great friends.

Jake wanted to put together a small group to play the clubs so my friend Dan Barrett and I rehearsed with him, made some demos, and played a few gigs. Jake kept telling me I should get back to New York, that's where things were happening. Then he helped to make it happen.

In 1982 Joe Bushkin was going to New York City to play at the Carlyle for three weeks. He wanted Johnny Smith to do the gig, but Johnny didn't want to spend more than a week in New York. So Jake said, "Joe, you should hire this guy Howard." Joe was one of the best piano players on the East Side, and this was one of the best clubs, but Jake's vote of confidence, along with a recommendation from another friend, got me the second and third weeks of the

(Clockwise from top left) Billy, Eleanor, Jake and Mary Hanna
outside Beaumont Street, 1937 | *Hanna family collection*

Camera shy Jake, who didn't have a picture in his yearbook, wears
a baseball cap and ducks his head at the top center of this picture
of the Dorchester Rompers baseball team in 1947 | *Hanna family
collection*

Jake plays with Jack LaSpina (bass),
Richard Boubelik (piano) and others at
Sheppard Air Force Base, 1952 |
Courtesy of Jack LaSpina

Jake Hanna, Regal Tip's
first endorser, 1961 |
*Courtesy of Carol Calato
of Regal Tip Drumsticks*

Jake, Woody Herman and Chuck Andrus at
Lennie's on the Turnpike, 1963 | *Courtesy of the
Salem State College archives*

Jake and Joe Venuti
swinging at Concord
1977 | *Courtesy of
Ellen Findlay Herdegen*

Jake was already packing them in at a 1972
drum clinic | *Hanna family collection*

Jake, Bob Yeager and the Bing drum head, 1978 | *Courtesy of Stan Keyawa*

Ron Della Chiesa interviews Jake in Boston, 1979 | *Courtesy of Ron Della Chiesa*

Judging by the plaid pants, Jake hadn't yet met Denisa at the time of this visit to his sister Eleanor and her family, 1979 | *Judge family collection*

No plaid in sight on Jake and Denisa's wedding day, 1984 |
Hanna family collection

Jake and Eiji Kitamura at a Concord Jazz recording session, 1981 | *Courtesy of Al Julian*

Jake and Buddy Rich in Stockholm, Sweden, 1986 | *Courtesy of Bob Bowlby*

Cal Collins, Jake and Ray Brown at the Concord Jazz Festival, 1982 | *Courtesy of Al Julian*

Carl Fontana, Dave Stone and Jake play at the Newport Beach Hyatt, 1993 |
Courtesy of Al Julian

The Mackinlay jug over Jake's head adds a nice touch to cocktail hour with Brian Lemon, Dave Green and Tony Shoppe at the Nellie Deane Pub in London, 1993 | *Courtesy of Dave Green*

Jake always had an appreciative feline audience when he practiced in the living room, 2000 | *Judge family collection*

Jeff Hamilton, Jake and Joe Calato at NAMM, 2005 |
Courtesy of Carol Calato

Dinner at Jake's with Charlie Watts, Jake, Rory Judge, Jim Keltner, 2006 |
Courtesy of Rory Judge

Jake and Warren Vaché on a
Concord gig in Antibes, 1979
| *Courtesy of Al Julian*

Jake and Warren Vaché at the Monterey Jazz Festival, 2009. Still
buddies after all these years | *Photo by Rory Judge*

gig. Joe returned the following January for 12 weeks and invited me back for that, too. That allowed me to pack up and move to New York City.

In 1984 Woody was going to play at the Rainbow Room with a small group. He didn't usually use a guitar player with that size group, but Jake told him to hire me. What a wonderful opportunity that was to play with Woody and Jake and a great rhythm section for a month.

Jake was hugely helpful in my career. He made it possible for me to move to New York and to play with some of the greatest players in the world. I developed confidence and got a certain prestige from working with such a great drummer. When I mentioned I played gigs with Jake, people really picked up their ears. I stayed in touch with Jake and Denisa and saw them whenever possible.

The main thing about Jake was that he was all music. There was sincerity and honesty in his playing, and if you played sincerely and honestly with him, he would like it and respect it. He had no tolerance for bullshit. When he played he was behind every note, there was no trying to put on airs. He was completely in service of the music, the beauty and the swing.

Jake was the most sincere, no-nonsense musician on any instrument, not just drums. Every note was from the heart and was full of integrity.

14

Root, Root, Root for the Home Team

Jake grew up in a city that was focused on sports and home to four major sports teams, the Boston Bruins, the Boston Celtics, the Boston Braves (who later moved to Wilwaukee and then Atlanta), and his beloved Boston Red Sox. It also had a multitude of passionately loyal fans, one of whom was Jake. The family finances didn't allow for many childhood visits to professional ballparks or basketball courts, though Jake did have one memorable trip to Fenway Park. But he followed sports on the radio, in the newspaper and played on the high school baseball and track teams. There were several sportswriters whose columns Jake and his friends read regularly, including one man who lived in the neighborhood and occasionally sent around tickets to some of the games.

At one point Jake thought he might give up drumming altogether to concentrate on sports, but his brother Billy, who was also a good baseball player, pointed out that while Jake had the potential to be a very good drummer, he would never go anywhere with sports.

Legions of jazz fans are grateful that Jake listened to his brother.

The following stories comes from Jake's friends and colleagues who knew his love of sports.

When I was young there was a conflict between my love for baseball and playing the drums. I was spending as much time playing baseball as I was playing the drums.

Jake Hanna

Jake's father, Jim Hanna, was a baseball fan and took him to Fenway Park for his first major league baseball game in 1939. The Red Sox were playing the New York Yankees, with Joe DiMaggio in centerfield. Years later, when Jake was playing with Jack Sheldon in Atlantic City, he and Denisa were having lunch at the Irish Pub. The Yankee Clipper was eating there, too, and asked to meet Jake. It turned out he was a big fan of Woody's. Jake always talked about meeting the great Yankee outfielder. It was a dream come true.

Al Julian

I met Joe. He was a real nice guy, a big fan of Woody. The manager came up to me at the bar in Atlantic City and said, "There's a guy over there who wants to meet you." And it's Joe DiMaggio. I said, "Hey Joe, how are you? I saw you with the Yankees at Fenway Park. Your brother was out there, it looked like an Italian Victory Garden with Dommie and Joe."

He asked me what was it was like to work for Woody. I said, "Exactly like it was for you to work for George Weiss."

"You mean you had to fight him for the money?"

"Yup."

"How'd you make out?"

"I never got it."

"Neither did I."

Jake Hanna as told to Rory Judge

Jake Hanna and I were friends since our teen years, and we both played on the Rompers baseball team. We went to different high schools, so we usually hung out evenings or weekends with the gang on the Dorchester Court House wall. Jake always had his drumsticks with him.

One Saturday afternoon during our sophomore year we were trying to decide who was the fastest runner in our gang. I said I was. Jake didn't agree and said he was faster. We soon decided to have a foot race to settle the friendly argument.

George Karalekas set up the race at nearby Franklin Field and appointed himself judge. He counted off a 50-yard dash on the dirt roadway, and then started us off. I flew out quickly, and at the halfway mark I was leading by a few steps. But Jake soon pulled even, ran by me, and won by about two yards. I was shocked and disappointed but I shook his hand and we talked about the race.

A few weeks later I learned from his schoolmates that Jake was on the high school track team and his specialty was the 50-yard dash. He neglected to mention that he was trained and ran track competitively for the school.

Bill Najjar

Jake did well in the 1,000, but he couldn't beat two of the guys, so he stopped running.

Fran Shaw

When we were young we played a lot of baseball games at Rogers Field and at Dorchester Town Field near where Jake lived. Jake was a great mimic, and did take-offs of his favorite baseball players. Night after night we'd watch him going through his ritual of winding up like Harry "the Cat" Brecheen. Jake would hold an imaginary bat in hand — in his left hand since Harry the Cat was a lefty — then he'd tug on his hat, pull down the visor, reach down to rub dirt on his hands, and then finally swing. Of course he mimed all this since he was usually doing it on the concrete grounds of the courthouse parking lot. He had every single detail down on the guy he was imitating and we always knew who it was because the great ones had such specific routines. He was so much fun to watch.

Eddie Miller

Jake was still doing those impressions of ballplayers later in life.

We had a ballclub in Boston in the late 1950s with me, Jake, Al Vega, Serge Chaloff and a few other guys. We played ballgames with other musicians. And he'd do those take-offs.

Joe Locatelli

One of Jake's idols was Stan Musial of the St. Louis Cardinals. He thought he was a great hitter. Bing Crosby was a baseball fan and part owner of Pittsburgh Pirates, so they had sports in common too.

Fran Shaw

Jake was a huge Red Sox fan and a real student of the game. In the fall of 2005 his beloved boys from Boston were once again in the hunt for the World Series, and many nights at his gigs I sat next to Jake between sets and watched the playoffs with him, even after "the Sox" were eventually eliminated from contention. He knew the game inside and out and was very knowledgeable about great players from various eras.

His face lit up when I told him I had been an all-star first baseman and captain of a citywide championship CYO (Catholic Youth Organization) team in my younger days, His first feature interview in Modern Drummer magazine was conducted in 1980 in the dugout of Dodger Stadium just after the L.A. team had deemed Mike Scioscia to be their No.1 one catcher. And Mike was being interviewed nearby. Even though that event happened more than three decades earlier, Jake was still enthusiastic as he told me how exciting it was to be sitting in that special place in the ballpark.

There were some magic moments during those playoffs, and when Jake was on stage and unable to watch the games, I would give him updates by flashing the score with my fingers. He made great, happy faces when things were going well for the Sox and very serious faces when things were not. As soon as each set was finished, we'd find a nearby television and continue watching the spectacle.

Jake was spellbound when he watched playoff baseball. He would cease holding court, freeze with his eyes riveted to the screen, and watch the high drama unfold. Once play was complete, he would speak again.

John King

Jake liked to watch boxing, and we used to talk on the phone about it a lot, especially when Canada had a couple of heavyweight boxers that did very well at the time.

Gilles Mongeau

If there was one thing that made Jake happy, it was watching the Boston Celtics beat the Los Angeles Lakers.

Rory Judge

Jake and Denisa were visiting Boston and came to my house to watch a Boston College football game. It was the one where Doug Flutie threw the "Hail Mary Pass." Jake was so excited he jumped off the couch.

Later we drove by Fenway Park so he could show it to Denisa. We went into the pro shop across the street, and I bought him a Red Sox training cap. For years after that I'd hear from people who said they'd just run into Jake and he was wearing that hat.

Al Julian

On a tour in 2000, we were riding by Fenway Park, and I said, "Hey, Jake. Look!" In case anyone didn't already know, Jake was a Red Sox fan through and through. We talked about the Sox's chances, and he said, "Ahh, by August they'll be dead last" Four years later, I was in Germany when the Sox finally won the World Series, breaking the almost 100-year-long "Curse of the Bambino." I wish I could have been in Los Angeles to see Jake's face.

Randy Reinhart

Patti and I came home about 11:30 at night from Dodger Stadium. As soon as we walked in the door, the phone rang. Kind of late to get a call. I picked up the phone, a little nervously.

Donald: Hello?

Voice: Don? Don Ross?

Donald: Yes?

Voice: It's Jake, Jake Hanna.

Donald: Hi, what's up?

Voice: You and Patti just got home from the ballgame, right?

Donald: Did you see us there?

Voice: Yeah, on TV. A million people saw you. They had the camera on you when you dropped the foul ball. Right in your hands, and you blew it, for Christ's sake. It came right to you.

With that, Jake hung up.

Donald and Patti Ross

`Round London Town

Brian Peerless

I first heard Jake live on a very short UK tour with Woody Herman in July 1964, although I knew his work from records including the excellent Newport All Stars album with Buck and the guys on Atlantic. I next heard him live when he toured the UK with a package entitled "Top Brass" in September and October 1967. It was at the end of this tour that I first met him as I worked in Dobell's Jazz Record Shop in London when they performed for six days at Ronnie Scott's Jazz Club in Soho. Jake would continue to call in at the shop in the following years while on his walks around town. He loved to walk everyday and, if based in London, would always walk to gigs from his hotel. Jake liked London, being able to wander around and have the odd pint of bitter. Some years later Kenny Davern and I ran into him and Denisa during their London honeymoon when they popped into the 100 Club in Oxford Street for a jazz benefit.

We got to be good friends in the late 1970s, and I always tried to hear him whenever he came to Britain. I would often ferry him to dates and came to loan him my drums, to which he took a liking, for some of his tours. This activity increased when I started organizing tours for American musicians at the instigation of Kenny Davern and Yank Lawson in the early 1980s. Jake would bring his cymbals and bass drum pedal and I would supply the rest. His instructions would be, "Don't bring any tom-toms, just your snare, hi-hat, bass drum and stands; otherwise they'll want me to play solos!" Jake kindly brought me pieces of kit, including a drum stool, which I still treasure, though I haven't played in many a year. He also brought over a calfskin drumhead and swopped it on my Ludwig snare drum and there it remains!

His kindness extended to many other friends he had in Britain. He even gave tips and lessons over the phone to a friend in the Isle of Man. Maybe it was the first drumming course by phone!

Over the years we traveled a lot of miles together listening to music and chatting during the journeys. Jake's enthusiasm and enjoyment of everything never diminished. I remember his excitement at some recordings I played him with Dave Tough on drums and how he would ask me to play the sides whenever he got into the car. He asked me if I could make a copy it for him to take home and "play for some of the guys to show them what it was all about." I was only too happy to do so.

We took in many venues around the country, often two- to three-week summer trips to take advantage of the festivals in Edinburgh, Brecon and Nairn, and to fit in work at clubs including the Concorde at Eastleigh in Hampshire, the Pizza Express Jazz Club in London, and clubs in Woking, Cambridge and Belfast. Jake had his fans everywhere we went and en route he always asked if I thought certain people would turn up. They usually did. In many cases he would have nicknames for them, which were always accurate, and you would know exactly who he was talking about! I was always amazed how he could remember so many people from all over the world.

Whenever I phoned him about coming over, we always had a great chat about everything, and he would ask what I had in mind. I would deliver an outline of the possible dates and the other musicians he would be playing with, British and American, and he would make noises at the other end like, "fine, excellent and well, you know, he's my man." Of course, I did know who he liked or probably would like! I only had to say Brian Lemon, Colin Purbrook, John Pearce, Dave Green, Alec Dankworth, or Roy Williams from the British camp to know I was on a winner. I always felt honored that he trusted my judgment. I also had a pretty good idea about who he didn't want to work with! I don't think he ever asked me how much it would pay. A good thing, as sometimes I didn't know!

Jake was a great supporter of young talent and always had open ears. During the years we put together many groups that featured his protégés Scott Hamilton, Howard Alden, and Harry Allen, young friends Ken Peplowski and

Jon-Erik Kellso, and old friends Yank Lawson, Bob Haggart, Ralph Sutton, Jack Lesberg, George Masso, John Bunch, Dave McKenna, Dick Wellstood, Jim Galloway, Michael Moore, Warren Vaché, Bucky Pizzarelli, and Kenny Davern along with his British buddies. It was fun and certainly never dull whenever Jake was involved.

Jake was the ideal man for our festivals as he loved to go off walking around Brecon or Edinburgh to see what was happening and in the course of his travels would chat with people on the street as well as listening to other players. He used to tell me he wanted to check out musicians so he could recommend players to any of his friends who were thinking of coming to Britain. He liked to have a little directory of musicians for every area he worked in the world. On one of our Edinburgh trips I asked what he'd been doing that particular day. He informed me with a chuckle he'd been to hear the Lightweight All Stars (a band billed as the Lighthouse All Stars).

During one period in London, Kenny Davern and I introduced him to a small Italian restaurant just off Russell Square, which delighted him. After that he wouldn't eat anywhere else, his motto being that once you found something good, stick with it. Needless to say, the staff loved him and his stories.

As we all know Jake had a fund of stories, which he loved to share with everybody! I remember one year when there was an accommodation shortage at Brecon and we stayed in Cardiff on the day before the festival. A friend of mine, John Lewis, who helped out with the driving, and I ran into Jake in the foyer. While we were deciding whether to stay in the hotel or go out for a drink, a couple stepped out of the lift and said hello. They were not jazz fans—in fact—I'm not sure whether they even liked music, but for the next 45 minutes Jake had them mesmerized with his tales of Bing, Harry James, and showbiz. At the end of it he'd gained two more life–long fans. He had a natural ability to make everyone feel they were a special friend.

I wish I could remember all the stories he told me, or all the quips he made. Many things he said sometimes pop into the mind at the most unexpected moments. A personal favorite is the comment he made about the well-oiled lady who was heaping praise on a less than talented group, "That's what comes of drinking on an empty head."

Some that I did witness on tour were as follows: at the dinner given for the 21st Anniversary World's Greatest Jazz Band in Belfast's City Hall in 1989 before the performance, I was seated next to Jake and when a very nervous young waitress brought the main course. Jake questioned her as to whether the meat was venison. The poor girl answered apologetically that it wasn't, to which he replied, "Thank goodness for that, I hate venison," and gave her a beam. She went away highly amused. At one of the Brecon years, Jake had a set with singer Jeannie Lamb, who appeared in a leopard print dress. Jake's aside to her was, "Hey Jeannie, did you shoot it yourself?" while he adjusted the drums. At the start of the same set, some technical trouble was encountered with the microphone, and Jeannie, to kill time, suggested to Jake that he tell a joke. Quick as a flash he came back with, "I thought this was it!" This resulted in much laughter from the audience, and more points scored by Jake. He was one of the most popular musicians ever to play at Brecon and we managed to organize it so that from the late 1980s he played there in some combination almost every year for nearly 20 years. He enthralled the audiences at every performance.

For me Jake was one of the all-time great jazz drummers whose company it was always a pleasure to be in. When we were putting together the cast list for our first Norwich Jazz Party in 2007, Jake was the first drummer called to participate. It was our honor to have him come play and totally enter into the spirit of the event. Not only did he hang out to listen to almost everything and chat with old friends including Jack Parnell and exchange some banter with surprise guest George Wein, he also provided two of the weekend's highlights. One was a trio set dedicated to Dave McKenna and led by Scott Hamilton with Rossano Sportiello in the piano chair. The other, on the last night, was an unscheduled addition to Rossano's solo set. A few minutes before the start, Rossano asked if he could ask Jake to play with him. Of course, the answer was yes, and Jake played with just a snare drum in a set that Rossano dedicated to his idol and Jake's longtime friend Ralph Sutton. The set rightly drew a standing ovation and was an object lesson in the art of playing with brushes. How privileged we were.

Unfortunately Jake couldn't come in 2008 as he was expecting to be on the other side of the world with Roberta Gambarini. We did however meet up at Brecon that summer when he came in for one day with Roberta. Scott Hamilton, John Pearce, Dave Green, Steve Brown, John Lewis and I crowded into a corridor backstage at the Theatr Brycheiniog and exchanged hugs and greetings. As always it was if we had been together all the time. This was, sadly the last time we met.

Jake was a rugged individual, a truly unique drummer with a sound and drive all his own whether playing with sticks or brushes, an asset to any group he ever played with, never giving less than 100 percent of himself, and a great guy to be with socially. My life has certainly been enriched by knowing him and having been lucky to spend time with him. We'll not see his like again. Thank you, Jake, for all the good times.

15

Jake, My Man

So what made Jake unique?

Did it have something to do with the notion of periodic phenomena, the way people are drawn together by special kinds of sounds or rhythms that they can imitate themselves?[25]

In certain styles of music, the persistent regularity of tempo is a very strong shaping force that surrounds and drives the entire piece. Jake's playing, in a sense, generated a kind of temporal grid that contained everything else. The improvisation, harmonies, sax solos, the choruses, all would still be there without the drums, but it wouldn't have the same compelling push that got it across to the audience. Your feet might tap if the band was playing without a rhythm section, but once the rhythm was added it would be like turning on a light in a dark room.

People at jazz concerts can feel the pulsation of music internally, and they

25 Everything I know about periodic phenomena I learned from a fascinating discussion with Professor Michael Rendish of the Berklee College of Music.

externalize it by tapping their feet. It connects them. Music was an important part of early cultures, and those sounds were incorporated into religious ceremonies to promote a feeling of camaraderie. Appreciating rhythmic music and responding to that pulsation can hold people together in a common temporal experience, an experience of time. And Jake was all about time.

People followed him as far back as his days in the drum and bugle corps. In the Air Force his bass drum set the regular tempo—left, right, left, right—that united hundreds of airmen into the ultimate shared temporal experience, marching on parade. That synchronization, an almost hypnotic rhythm, can open the mind to suggestion and provide a key to getting into the human consciousness. Any good solid drummer who plays with a straight beat and a good groove can evoke that response in people.

Was this Jake's secret? Was his ability to keep good time, combined with his precise comedic timing, a way of bringing people together in a rhythmically, and possibly even a hypnotically induced experience of fascination and hilarity, designed to create legions of fans around the world?

As my mother often responded to my requests for information about Jake's childhood, "I have absolutely no idea."

But maybe it was.

These stories are tributes from friends, fans and fellow musicians.

Jake was always very sensitive to the feelings of his close friends and was quick with a quip or joke to lighten up a bad mood.

Once, Jake and I were among many musicians performing at a jazz party. We all had finished for the evening and were fraternizing in the green room/musicians' lounge. Jake's dear friend, the great pianist Ralph Sutton, was in a dour mood and blue about something. Jake tried to cheer him up, but nothing seemed to work. There was some music playing on a tape player in the background, so Jake stood up, turned up the volume and began to dance. The image of Jake Hanna trying to dance was funny enough but soon he began to add some silly motions and some up and down tidal waves with his belly. Well, Ralph began to smile, and then he began to laugh.

Pretty soon he was nearly doubled over, with tears streaming down his face from laughing so hard. Jake finished his performance, and Ralph played magnificently the rest of the week.

Butch Miles

I must have known Jake for more than 50 years. He was one of the eminent jazz artists of the time and really made that Herman band fly. I admired his work, and he was a lot of fun to be with.

I would run into him all around the country. I happened to be in the Pro Drum Shop in Hollywood a few years ago and suddenly insults started flying at me from behind the drums. It was Jake. I said, "Oh, we must still be friends, because you're still insulting me."

Vic Firth

Jake and I were hanging out after a concert and ended up at a club where drummer Danny D'Imperio was playing with his band. He saw Jake and acknowledged him as "not just any old Tom-Tom, Dick Dick or Harry Harry!"

For once Jake had no comeback.

Jim Galloway

A guy called me up one day, said his name was Jake Hanna, said he needed an appraisal on his house. I knew him from his work with Bing and Rosie, and I thought, *Wow, Jake Hanna is calling me*.

Several years later, a few of us were at the Pro Drum Shop in Hollywood one Christmas, and Jake was firing off stories like an Uzi. I said to Jeff Hamilton, "We've got to get this guy and let him tell his stories." So seven of us went to the L.A. Athletic Club for the first "Jake Hanna Lunch." We had to work out schedules around Jeff and Joe, but it was worth it. We'd bullshit, tell stories, and laugh a lot.

We're still meeting all these years later, but now there's a vacant chair at the table.

I used to drive Jake to the Christmas party at the Pro Drum Shop, and Bob Yeager's widow used to call me "Hoke," after the Morgan Freeman character in "Driving Miss Daisy." Now when I see her I say, 'There's no Hoke this year."

Bill Selditz

Jake took a liking to me in the late `60s when I was the house drummer at the Half Note in New York City where I played mostly with Al Cohn and Zoot Sims, and we spent many hours together as he told his stories and we talked about drumming. He liked my touch on the ride cymbal especially, and I confessed I probably stole it from listening to him on all those records. I became popular in the studio scene, and when I met up with Paul McCartney, my jazz career somehow got lost.

Years after leaving McCartney, I was living in L.A. when Zoot came to town for a gig. The whole New York contingent turned out. Jake was holding court when I showed up, and to no surprise had a few things to say. He announced to the guys, "You remember Denny from the New York days? He left jazz to play with a Beatle. Hey Denny, show them your money," which he said in a loving way, knowing that I got stiffed on the gig. We all had a good laugh.

Jake will be missed by all who knew him, by all who knew his sense of humor, and by those who heard him play just one time. That's all it took. I loved that guy and am sorry that I didn't spend more time with him in L.A. in his last years. Running into him at Pro Drum was always a great treat, and took me back to the finest times of my life in the Apple.

Jake Hanna ... the man, the legacy, the Best!

Denny Seiwell

You never knew what to expect from Jake. Like the time when he got a carpenter to cleverly cut his bass drum and his floor tom in half to telescope the other drums and close it with airplane clips. It saved money and space while traveling. And the drums sounded fine.

He had an undying passion for the Boston Red Sox. I once sent him a sports magazine with Ted Williams on the cover, and he had to tell EVERYone about it. After that I'd run into people who'd say, "Oh, Jake told me you gave him that." Then he met my wife and found out that she had done Red Sox commercials and knew Ted Williams. After that, no one else could get a word in for an hour!

We had these drummer lunches — we called them the Jake Hanna lunches — where he'd hold court, and we'd laugh so hard we'd get a pain in the belly. I arrived at one of the lunches with some news: "Lou Bellson broke his hip." Jake immediately cracked, "I'm surprised he didn't break two at once" — a reference to Bellson's playing two bass drums. We all cracked up while I tried to protest, "That was cold," between laughs.

He was a character. How many people tell Jake Hanna stories? Every drummer I know has one.

I was proud to be Jake's friend and will miss his great story telling as much as his superb drumming.

Ed Shaughnessy

I first played with Jake in 1967 on Woody's band and later in California in small groups. When I played with him I said it was like "riding on waves — you would just float along!"

One time he told me something important: "When you work for amateurs, you get treated like an amateur." I can't tell you how many times since then that I've heard that in my head. Maybe you have to be a musician, and go through all the ridiculous things we've had to go through, and all the ways we've been treated by people who don't know any better, to be able to understand that statement. I've never heard anyone else say that, and I've never read it anywhere. The only time I ever heard that short, profound statement was from Jake. I've had experiences since which made me think of what he said.

Roger Neumann

I used to see Jake play in New York with Woody Herman, but I didn't meet him until years later, when we were both playing at the West Texas Jazz Party. All he used was a bass drum, a snare drum and a cymbal; that was it. But you couldn't tell how small the kit was because of how well he played. We played lots of sets together and always had fun, on stage and at the parties in band room till 4 in the morning. He was always breaking everyone up. I like the story about Buddy Rich's funeral when Mel Torme was walking around with a clipboard telling everyone he had the rights to Buddy's story, and Jake told him, "Make sure you remember to mention Buddy's name!"

He was sensational to work with; he always knew what he was doing.

Bucky Pizzarelli

Besides being a fabulous swinging drummer, Jake was not a lazy drummer. He was always on the ball with his playing. As a piano player I would often encounter drummers playing as hard behind me as they would with the trumpet player preceding my chorus. Jake would always take the trouble to put down his sticks, pick up his brushes and swing just as hard, but not as loud, behind the horn. His solos and fours also were as humorous as his wit would allow.

Johnny Varro

I had an interesting experience with Jake in Los Angeles sometime in the 1970s. Herbie Mickman was doing an appearance before the Bass Club with two basses plus Jake, and he called me up to say the other bass canceled and could I play. I reminded him I don't play the bass, but he said he decided to do a trio instead. We started playing, then all of sudden Jake sounds like Roy Haynes. He did something totally different from what he was going to play. It was amazing.

Another time we were playing at a jazz party with Flip Philips and Jake on drums. The time came for the fours and one of us plays the first fours, then we expect Jake to play the next fours but he didn't, so the other sax player did his. We went on and later I asked him why he didn't play. He said, "I wanted them to hear the difference." That's pretty insightful, because when the horn plays fours and the drummer doesn't play his in between, the connecting fabric is gone.

Lew Tabackin

Every time I saw Jake at a jazz party or festival, he excited the silliness in me to come out. He also excited the serious in me to be still and listen to his unbelievable, tasteful drumming closely, so I wouldn't miss a thing! He was — and *is* — the best ever. On a German concert tour that lasted about two weeks, I was fortunate to sit with Jake and Denisa every day on the ride to our next concert. The Jake stories were non-stop, and on the five or six hour rides I feared I might need to ask the driver to stop so I could pee and catch my breath from laughing so hard. His incredible detail in story telling was woven so beautifully, as if he were a great sculptor or painter.

Around 1990 at the Triangle Jazz Party in Kingsport, Tenn., some of the musicians were asked to come a day early to do school programs. Many of us said yes, including Jake. The director, Steve Blades, had a big party at his house the night before, and we were — let's say — over served. The next morning as we gathered to be driven to the school programs, Steve told us we had four schools to do. Jake responded, "Four, Steve? Hell no! I got one in me, but not four. I feel awful. I gotta go back to bed." Steve told him to see how he felt after the first one. Of course, Jake did all four programs and actually spent extra time with the kids at the last school. The kids all gathered around him as he taught them different ways of holding the sticks, how to hit the cymbals for the best sound, and so on. He was holding court. We couldn't tear him away. It was beautiful to witness.

Jake was, and still is, an extremely important person in my life. We even shared the same April 4th birthday. I felt so lucky. I think of him often and, when I do, my heart lights up. I am honored to have known him, played music with him, and hung out with him. He will certainly live on forever.

Eddie Erickson

I first heard about Jake through the drummer Hal Smith, whom I frequently worked with. He was one of his biggest fans, so Jake's name came up often.

The Triangle Jazz Party was the first jazz party I ever went to. It was star-studded, and Jake Hanna was there, and I think that's when I first met him. He loved to tell stories and laugh, but he really loved playing. It was always a pleasure to hear him play, to share the stand with him. He'd say to me, "You've got it, you sing great." Lots of musicians aren't that friendly to chick singers, so I treasured his praise. I always felt so honored when I saw Jake in the audience, smiling and being supportive.

Once he was interviewed by Modern Drummer Magazine, and they asked him if there were any groups on the scene that he liked. He mentioned my group BED (Becky, Eddie and Dan) and afterwards laughed and said, "There's no drummer in that band." We thought it was very nice for a "drum-less" group to be mentioned in *Modern Drummer*.

Jake was a true jazz musician in the way he lived and socialized. He had that great smile and oh, his wonderful playing.

We had lots of fun with Jake and Denisa. I felt they really took such good care of each other.

Rebecca Kilgore

Jake had a great ear for tuning drums. In my humble opinion, Shelley Manne was the best at that, but Jake came close.

I had a fast tempo, so I needed people who could keep up with me, and Jake could. He had good judgment and a good ear. He could tune and play soft without losing his intensity. That's some-thing that comes with training. He was a traditional player — he decided at some point that's what he wanted to be. He wasn't going to play abstract, he just wanted to have a good beat and swing.

I have such great respect and a warm feeling for him. He was a remarkably warm person and a rare, great player.

Toshiko Akiyoshi

I wish I could say that I remember the moment I first became aware of Jake Hanna, or even the first time I heard and watched him in person, but the truth is I can't. These days the old memory isn't what it should be, but in a way that's only appropriate: Jake's subtle swing was something that crept up on you rather than mak-ing a big crash-bang immediate impact.

What I can clearly remember was my joy in the mid-1970s, first to discover the Concord record label was still recording the kind of small-group swing that I loved, and then to gradually become aware that one Jake Hanna seemed to be effectively the Concord "house" drummer. He was on those great early Concords by Scott Hamilton (himself a revelation: a young guy who played like Ben Webster!), Warren Vaché, Maxine Sullivan and Flip Phillips. Best of all was a wonderful LP, "Live At Concord," recorded at the 1975 Concord Summer Festival by the Hanna-Fontana Band with Jake, Carl Fontana, Dave McKenna, Bill Berry, Heb Ellis, Plas Johnson and Herb Mickman. What a great, swinging session! I will always remember being moved by Jake's spoken introduction to "I Found A New Baby," as he dedicated the number to Zutty Singleton, who had died five days earlier.

In fact, it was that little tribute to Zutty that alerted me to the fact that not only was Jake a contemporary master of swing drumming, but he also, quite clearly, had a keen and astute appreciation of the great players who'd gone before. Listen closely to Jake and you'll hear hints of Big Sid, Davey Tough and Jo Jones. I read a Down Beat interview with George Wettling in the late 1950s or early `60s in which George is asked who is his favorite contemporary drummer. He replies something like, "Jake Hanna, because he plays like me!" Actually, I think George was flattering himself. Jake didn't play like anyone except himself, though he sort of hinted at many of the earlier drum pioneers. George, I understand, gave Jake a cymbal, just like Baby Dodds had given George a cymbal many years earlier.

When did I first get to see and hear Jake "in the flesh?" I can't remember. I know for sure that I saw him and had a brief, but highly enjoyable conversation, at 'The First Swinging Jazz Party" in Blackpool (UK), 2000. My main recollection of that event was a wonderful pickup group consisting of Jake, Dan Barrett, John Bunch, Michael Moore and either Jon-Eric Kellso or Warren Vaché (memory says it was Vaché, but the program I've recently dug out says Kellso). Anyway, I remember thinking, *if Eddie Condon was alive today, this would be his band.*

But I think I'd seen Jake before that: I certainly remember a session at my local Birmingham (UK) Jazz Festival, where he played in a pickup group with trumpeter Randy Reinhart and Brits Brian Lemon (piano) and Len Skeat (bass), while local drummer Al Sharpe and I exchanged glances of simple wonder and amazement. I remember that Jake had a minimal kit of just bass drum, snare (no toms), hi-hat and a couple of ride cymbals, one of which was an amazing china-boy that really drove Reinhart when he took a second chorus. I remember saying to Al Sharpe, "This is a lesson in 'less is more.' "

My favorite memory of Jake, however, is probably at the Pizza Express club in Soho, London around that time. The band included Jake, Kenny Davern, Marty Grosz, Ralph Sutton and, as I recall, the British bass player Dave Green. In the audience were Warren Vaché; Beryl Bryden, the veteran British singer (and institution); jazz writer (and another institution) Jim Godbolt; and several other legendary figures from the Brit jazz scene. The band swung like the proverbial clappers, as you'd expect with that rhythm section, while Davern wailed above them. I turned to my partner and said, "As far as I'm concerned, this is heaven; from now on the rest of my life will be an anti-climax."

Maybe that was a slight case of hyperbole, but only a very slight case!

Thank you, Jake, for some of the most wonderful musical moments of my life.

Jim Denham

Jake had a joyous beat. That's what it's all about in jazz — a joyous, beautiful feeling.

Joe Lovano

Jake Hanna kept us all honest. When he was around at jazz parties, he didn't let anyone get away with any bullshit. I treasure the time I spent with him. I learned a lot from him and never stopped laughing around him. I was honored to have played vibes with him a few times and to hear him play drums many times. He was the greatest.

Chuck Redd

Jake was always upbeat. I rarely saw him upset or mad at anyone. What a great laugh. He was a great man and drummer.

His spirit is one to admire and will live on long after the man himself. I carry Jake in my heart forever and am lucky to have met such a soul.

Joe Romersa

I heard a lot about Jake before we actually met, so I immediately liked him and sensed we had similar senses of humor. We were friends from that point on. My wife Marie reminded me recently about the time we went to one of Jake and Denisa's chili parties after the Sweet and Hot Jazz Festival and how Jake and I sat up until 5 in the morning telling stories and breaking each other up.

At the 2009 Sweet and Hot, Jake wasn't well, so he didn't play all the sets he usually did. On the last day Wally Holmes and I were sitting together listening to a flashy young drummer who was making a lot of noise. Wally pointed out that he really wasn't playing with the rest of the band. A bit later Jake came up and began to play simply, with great time. About 8 bars in, Wally and I looked at each other and said, "That's the way you're supposed to do it." I'll never forget that.

He was a wonderful player, an original, a true jazz player, someone we can all learn from.

We liked him a lot and miss him a lot. It was great to have that friendship for all those years.

Frank DeVito

Jake Hanna represents the true spirit of the meaning of "Jazz Drummer." I admired him as a person and musician. He will be missed.

Remo Belli

I loved singing with Jake. We'd sit around the living room and do Rodgers and Hart — Jake always called him "Larry Hart" — and then talk about songs. He'd say, "Do you know this one," and then he'd start singing in his beautiful voice. I'd ask him what the tempo was, and of course, he knew the perfect tempo for every song. He knew exactly where it lay, and he'd tell me why. I was so lucky to have that experience with him. Sometimes he'd accompany himself with the brushes, but when he sang full out it was really something. He'd talk about who wrote it, or who sang it, or who did the best job on it, or what the tempo should be, or that it shouldn't be a blues song but something else instead.

Terrie Richards

Jake was always about the music, all the time. His very presence made any event much more musical. If you were going to play
with him you knew the music would *have* to happen. It was never
about the gig or the money, just about an immediate relationship
to the music. When you played with him you always turned to him
to see if the music was okay.

He was absolutely one of a kind. People fit patterns. You usually
end up with people like you, but you rarely run into someone who
is one of a kind. With Jake, knowing you were going to see him was
always a special thing.

He was totally his own person and stayed that way, never
veered from that.

Wally Holmes

The first time I heard Jake play was on my Woody Herman records.

The first time I saw him play live was at the Metropole Club in
New York. The band used to play behind the bar in a big long line,
with Bill Chase on trumpet and Sal Nistico on sax. After that I saw
Jake on stage, mainly with the Woody Herman band.

Years later he came to see me in Los Angeles when Dave Green
and I were playing in a Charlie Parker tribute. That was the first time
I actually met him, was able to say "Hello, Jake Hanna, how are
you." I've loved him ever since.

Then I met up with him much later in Los Angeles. Whenever I
was in town, Jim Keltner and I went round to visit. He and Denisa
invited us to dinner which was very kind of them.

The last time I saw him was in Japan when he was playing with
Roberta Gambarini. He was fantastic, he had no drums on stage,
but the sound was incredible. He was wonderful, and we had a
great time. Denisa was a bit worried about him taking such a long
flight, but I rang her and said he was fine.

Jake didn't have much of an effect on me in my formative years
because I never saw him then. But later, when I went round to his

house in Los Angeles, just talking with him had an effect on me. He taught me a lot without saying anything, which was his way of doing things. He'd get a cymbal out and start playing. He taught me that time was the right thing to do. When I saw him play with Roberta, that's what he played, he just played time on the cymbal. It was magical. That's kind of what he did for me.

He gave me a DVD of him with the Woody Herman band, which is the way I remembered him playing. It was a live television show with Sal Nistico, and it had amazing tempos. He was a fantastic drummer, never a big showoff but he had it all covered. To hold the Woody Herman band on live television, playing things like "Caldonia" with those tempos, that was really something else. He thought highly of that performance because he loved Sal Nistico, that's what he said.

Jake gave me one of his cymbals, and then I bought a snare drum that had been one of his. I treasure those in my collection.

Charlie Watts

It was the greatest thing in the world to be around Jake. He was a sweetheart with an unbelievable sense of humor, so warm to everyone he loved and not reluctant to let people know if he didn't like them. He was amazingly intelligent, and his observations were just incredible.

His musicality was beyond belief; nobody swung harder than Jake. Singers loved him because he was right there with phrasing, and so dynamic. He was one of the really unsung giants of this music. Musicians knew it but the public never really recognized it because he was so subtle. He didn't call attention to himself; he was busy taking care of the music.

I was working with Roberta Gambarini in early 2006 when a gig in Japan came up suddenly. Her drummer wasn't available so Howard Alden suggested she try Jake. I said "Absolutely! If he's available, he's hired." I called him, and he said, "Yeah, I can do that."

I told him, "This is her first gig over there so the money won't be great," but he said, "That's okay, if you say she can sing, I'm in." I said, "She can really sing; after Sarah, Ella and Carmen left us, this is the best singer I've heard since them." I told him what the money was and he said, "That ain't bad." We went to Japan with no time for a rehearsal so Roberta didn't meet him until we got to the gig, · and even then there was barely time for a sound check. Of course, from the first tune she fell in love with him. She didn't want to work with anyone else, and she hardly did as long as he was available.

Later that same year Jake was playing with Roberta at the Vic in Santa Monica. Roy Hargrove was in town and came over to sit in. Jake's playing just floored him. He came over and asked, "Who is that drummer? He's perfect!" Now Jake's profile is this Irish look-ing, 70-ish guy from Boston, not the typical kind of drummer most people would have predicted Roy would lock onto. But Roy's a guy who can appreciate swing, and he was flabbergasted when I said who it was. He said, "Oh, I know his name," but he didn't have any idea this guy was the Jake Hanna he'd heard.

I loved Jake from the bottom of my soul.

Larry Clothier

About half hour or so and after Larry talked to Jake, Roberta turned to me in the car and said Jake had to talk to me before he would accept the gig in Japan. So I called him, and he said, "Who is this broad? Can she sing? If she stinks I don't want to have to buy my own ticket to come home from Japan!" I said, "Trust me, you'll love her." After that he accepted the gig, and was quite happy once he started playing with her.

Howard Alden

My father loved big band music, and I first heard Jake on his Woody Herman records. I knew he was Bing's and Rosemary's drummer, and I admired his drumming.

After I moved to the U.S., I mentioned to Howard Alden that I needed a drummer for a gig in Tokyo. I told him my favorite drummer in the world was Jake Hanna but didn't know if he would want to go out on a tour. Howard took out his cell phone and gave me Jake's phone number, but I was a bit self-conscious, so my manager called him. They talked about the setup and Larry asked if he would need tom-toms? "Why would I need tom-toms?" Jake asked him. "Is she planning to sing jungle music?" I felt like I had gotten my first Jake Hanna-ism.

I was fascinated by Jake's sound. He was one of the last really great artists who knew the disappearing art of tuning the drums. His tuning was amazing and generated a certain type of sound, in addition to the rhythm feel. It was exquisite, particularly reactive to the soloist. In terms of sound, it's not only a matter of rhythm and accent; it's also a matter of sound and melody on the drums. Toshiko and I talked about this during a sound check in Japan while Jake was tuning his drums. She agreed he had not lost the art of tuning the drums in that certain way.

It was thrilling to play with Jake. He was the perfect drummer for me, for singers, so tasteful. He was an artist and played the drums from an artist's standpoint, not just as an accompanist. Swing was his thing; he could stir it up with minimum effort. Also, for me, the feeling he would come up with in ballads was fantastic. I consider myself blessed to have had the opportunity to work so much with him, to tour all over the world together.

And then there was the person, a fascinating source of stories, evoking a world of the past, of musicians and boxers and the many people he had met. Roy Hargrove sometimes toured with us and came to play with us because he loved working with Jake. We had a great time on the road. Jake was infallible in the way he played, someone you could always count on musically. He was always following you in every possible nuance. That's the mark of a great artist, getting the maximum result with the minimum effort.

It was great to watch him play. His physical attitude was so relaxed; when you looked at him you didn't see any strain. At a Lionel Hampton festival, I went to Jeff Hamilton's master class where he talked about the importance of swing and having a good time and being relaxed. I looked at pictures of my favorite drummers — Elvin Jones, Philly Joe, Jake Hanna — they had different expressions, but they all looked, relaxed, they didn't have clenched jaws. I remember Jeff citing Jake as an example.

His getting sick left us in dismay. We were so worried. I stayed in touch with Denisa and at one point it seemed like he was getting better. Then I got a text one evening saying he had become critical. I called Denisa right away and he was in and out of consciousness, but she said he would be able to hear me. She held the phone up to his ear and I spoke to him. I was so glad I had a chance to tell him I loved him, to tell him how much I loved them. She called me about 15 minutes later to say he had just passed.

Jake made excellence a priority. It was his lifestyle. It was about playing better all the way to the end. With him it was innate; he was born with a certain way of hearing music. It was never just about his prowess in playing the instrument itself but about his total ability to hear, his total musical intelligence. Playing good and playing great was the result of his ability to hear, his taste, his musical intelligence. He wasn't just a great instrumentalist, but a great musician.

I learned so much from working with him. It was great to know him as a person and to know him and Denisa together.

Roberta Gambarini

16

The Sticks are Stilled

The phone rang one Friday evening as I prepared to watch the Olympic Opening Ceremonies. It was Feb 12, 2010, and Uncle Jake had died at 4:15 in a Los Angeles hospital. My memory of the Athlete's Parade that evening will forever be blurred, as I watched it through teary eyes.

Jake had always seemed so healthy. He was plagued by occasional bouts of vertigo, but managed them with a typically Jake flair. Once he had just finished a gig when he had an attack and got so dizzy he started to fall off the stage. Someone grabbed him and helped him to a chair. He looked up to thank his rescuer and discovered it was Clint Eastwood.

But he'd been sick for more than a year, and no one could figure out what ailed him. He kept playing, with gigs in Monterey in March 2009 and at the Sweet & Hot Festival that September. In October he had to cancel a trip to NYC for a recording date. He was eventually diagnosed with mastocytosis, where the overproduction of his body's mast cells caused liver and lymphatic damage. Eventually his blood wouldn't clot properly. Multiple transfusions tried to resolve the internal bleeding but after a while that wasn't enough, and by then he was too frail for other procedures.

During the last months of Jake's life, I spent as much time with him as I could. I wanted to just be with him and help out as much as possible, but I ended up getting the lessons of a lifetime.

We talked a lot about drums and music, and the conversation inevitably turned into a lesson. We would listen to old jazz records and talk about the drummers, then he would have me play, and he would show me things on his drum pad or hi-hats and critique me. He could be both complimentary and critical. If I played it wrong he would stop me and push me to get it right. When I got it right he would encourage me to keep going. One time I was practicing on his pad in the living room, and he yelled from the back room that I was playing it wrong. I played it again, and I heard, "No, it's still wrong." One more time and I finally heard, "Yeah that's it, you got it." He was sick in bed and in pain but still paid attention.

He talked about having me spend a couple of weeks working with him and practicing together four or five hours a day. He told me he wanted to get serious about teaching me and wanted me to do the same. We started making plans, but we ran out of time.

Even at the very end, during that last week when he was so sick in the hospital, he would still talk about drums and music with me. That wasn't surprising for the man who lived and breathed them.

Rory Judge

I visited Uncle Jake in the hospital in late January. He was sitting there, glasses on, newspaper in hand, scowling at the television and making sardonic comments about the basketball score. He made me laugh, as usual. It was about two weeks before he died. In retrospect, it seemed surreal that someone so close to death could be so full of life.

Brigid Judge

Denisa was playing some CDs in Jake's hospital room just before he died. He wasn't conscious, but the nurses said that he was able to hear them. So the music of Dave McKenna and Roberta Gambarini eased him on his way.

Rory Judge

Jake's sister Eleanor was on the West Coast shortly after Jake's passing, and we got together for our own little tribute. Jake's family, my daughter Cecilia and her husband, Rich, and I gathered to share stories and raise our glasses to him. It seemed fitting to invite Doug Kassell and Lisa Patten, who live in our town. Jake was Marian McPartland's drummer for many years, and Doug is her drummer grandson.

Jake will always be in our memories and in our hearts.

Merrilee Trost

Stew Jackson called me as soon as he heard that Jake had died. He said he would bring the Woody Herman Band to play for his memorial, whenever we scheduled it. He flew Frank Tiberi and all the guys out for it.

Denisa Hanna

On April 18, 2010 the music community got together for "A Celebration of Jake" at Catalina's Bar & Grill in North Hollywood. More than 200 people attended. It was a great sendoff for Jake and a great opportunity for people who didn't get to see him near the end of his life. Wally Holmes stepped in as master of ceremonies on about 24 hours' notice and was his usual wonderful self. Howard Alden and Polly Podewell opened with a beautiful rendition of "Thanks for the Memories" with special lyrics Polly wrote for the occasion. Next came the Woody Herman Orchestra with Jeff Hamilton on drums, and they really swung — the joint was jumping. Many of Jake's favorites were on stage that afternoon including

Dave Stone, Harry Allen and John Allred. A short film about Jake followed that had people laughing and crying ... I think there may have been more crying actually. Then Roberta Gambarini took the stage with her Trio: Tamir Hendelman, Chuck Berghofer and Joe La Barbera on drums. Jake loved playing with her, and his very last recording session was on her "So In Love" album. She was amazing. What a great way to close the show.

It was a loose and easy gathering, no speeches or heaviness, just great stories about Jake, incredible jazz, afternoon cocktails and food. I think Jake might have liked that.

Rory Judge

We wanted to hang a picture of Jake on the stage for the Catalina's tribute but couldn't find anything to hold it up. I thought of using dental floss since that's how I hang thing up at my house and Rory said there was a drugstore around the corner. It did the trick. I couldn't decide if Jake would have been impressed by my resourcefulness—he was, after all, known for creative repairs to his equipment — or if he would have faulted me for not planning ahead.

Scott Thorburn

Jake wanted his ashes buried in Dorchester with his brother, Billy, so I began to plan an event at Florian Hall in Dorchester, about a mile away from the house on Beaumont Street where he was born. One particularly hectic morning I was rushing around town juggling errands and phone calls when I remembered I was supposed to pick up a registered letter at the post office. I went to the wrong branch first, then to the right one, where I waited in line, showed my ID, signed — then printed — my name and address in two different places, then finally was handed a package, and as I wondered what could possibly require such careful scrutiny, I looked at the box and saw it was from the Inglewood Cemetery/Mortuary and realized it was ... Uncle Jake's ashes.

I stopped rushing, and reverently carried the box home in one of my reusable grocery bags, placed it on top of my entertainment center—that seemed a fitting place — and played him a brand new Becky Kilgore CD that also arrived in the mail that day, though much less dramatically.

Maria Judge

I just got in from the "Jake Hanna Hometown Celebration," at Florian Hall. It was a hell of a time. A bunch of super musicians had a two-hour jam session and told stories about working with Jake. These guys have played with Woody Herman, Tommy Dorsey and with big bands all over the place. Harry Allen on the tenor sax played "Stardust," a tune he said Jake hated. All the guys—Harry, Howard Alden on guitar, Joel Forbes on bass, Jim Gwin on drums, Randy Reinhart and Warren Vaché on trumpets — were masterly, as was the singer Becky Kilgore. They came from the West Coast, New Jersey, New York City and from Upstate New York. They were great.

Dave Kenney, 8/8/2010 e-mail to his Dorchester friends

The sound system in the Florian Hall video projection unit wasn't working properly so we couldn't get any sound for the Jake video tribute. I rushed to up to the Staples on the corner for an adapter, then Jake's nephew, Joe, and I jury-rigged the podium microphone and stuck it up against the tiny speaker on my laptop to broadcast the sound. The mike was lying on the floor and I was surprised you couldn't hear footsteps as people walked around the room. Again I wondered what Jake would have thought.

Scott Thorburn

When I went up to Dorchester for Jake's tribute, I visited the cemetery where his ashes were buried. Now whenever I have a gig near Boston, I go back there and drink a beer while I visit him.

Warren Vaché

CODA

Ron Della Chiesa

Jake was like one of the great masters. Just as you didn't know how Raphael or John Singer Sargent created their masterpieces, you don't really know how Jake got that sound. It was unique, unmistakable, like a subtle splash in the ocean. I can hear it in my head. He never overplayed. He was always there, and you knew it was Jake. He had the innate ability to play so subtly behind everything, but to be strong at the same time. Subtlety and strength, that's an amazing combination. He had impeccable taste.

I first met him at the North Shore Music Theater in Beverly, Mass, when he was playing with a Woody Herman revival band that included Nat Pierce and Dave McKenna and some of the other guys who'd been with Woody. Dave introduced us at the intermission, and we hit it off. Then I'd see him later when he was playing in town with Scott Hamilton and others.

I had a great relationship with Jake. I looked forward to his trips to Boston because I knew it would be extraordinary to hear him. Whenever he came to Boston, Al Julian brought him by the studio. and then he'd sit there patiently and listen as Jake talked about everything. He had done and seen so much. He was on the first Concord recording, and, of course, was instrumental in the label's success because he brought so many musicians there. I'm sure he put a lot of those sessions together so he had a powerful impact as a producer as well as a musician and raconteur.

Jake was a natural storyteller. He had all these stories in his head and could tell them so well. I think some of that must have come from the time he spent on the road. The ratio of travel time to playing time for musicians is probably about 3 to 1. So when you're not playing you read, or listen to the radio or tell stories.

Jake was big everywhere. All he had to do was get up there and start talking. He would have made a good politician—I can just picture him on the City Council. He didn't suffer fools gladly. He would have told it like it is. He and Ruby Braff were similar in that respect. Neither of them held back.

217

The last time I heard him play was at a jazz club in Los Angeles with Scott and Ross Tompkins. I could hear from outside that it was Jake. He came over at the break, sat down, and we picked up where we'd left off the last time. He had lots of stories about Dave McKenna, and Ruby Braff and Joe Venuti were two other musicians who came up again and again in his stories.

I consider Jake to be in a special class. In the history of jazz percussion he was right up there with Jo Jones and the other great drummers he admired. He did so much, played with big bands, with his own bands: Hanna-Fontana was one of the great bands.

Jake could do it all.

CONTRIBUTORS

1. **Toshiko Akiyoshi** has been playing the piano since before she and Jake were Berklee classmates
2. **Howard Alden** and his jazz guitar have played and recorded with Joe Bushkin, Ruby Braff, Warren Vaché, Woody Herman, Kenny Davern, Dizzy Gillespie and George Van Eps
3. **Harry Allen** and his tenor saxophone have recorded extensively, performed around the world, and co-lead The Harry Allen–Joe Cohn Quartet
4. **Bill Allred** is a jazz trombonist, bandleader, staff musician at Walt Disney and former member of the Wild Bill Davison Jazz Band
5. **John Allred,** the third-generation Allred trombonist, played with the Woody Herman Orchestra and Toshiko Akiyoshi, has recorded and performed at jazz festivals, on Broadway and around the world
6. **Joe Ascione** has been playing the drums since age two, was Buddy Rich's roadie when he was a teenager, and has appeared on more than 60 recordings
7. **Dan Barrett** is a trombonist, cornetist and arranger who led a quintet with Howard Alden, served as music director for Arbors Records in Clearwater, Fla, and put the "D" in BED
8. **Vic Barrientos** is a free-lance professional musician/drummer from East Los Angeles
9. **Patty Tierney Belforti** and her family lived next door to Eleanor Hanna Judge's family in Hull, Mass
10. **Remo Belli** is the founder of Remo Drums
11. **Dick Berk** is a jazz drummer and bandleader who founded the Jazz Adoption Agency
12. **Lee E. Berk** is the former President of Berklee College of Music
13. **Betty Berry** and her husband, Bill, were great friends of Jake and Denisa's, and Bill and Jake worked together on the Woody Herman and Merv Griffin bands
14. **Jim Bono** is a high school friend of Jake's from Dorchester
15. **Richard Boubelik** played with Jake in the Air Force Band
16. **Bob Bowlby** is a saxophonist who played with Buddy Rich, Tommy Dorsey and Artie Shaw
17. **Roger Brown** is President of Berklee College of Music and a drummer
18. **Roy Burns** is a big band, studio, and jazz drummer and teacher
19. **Maria Bushkin Stave** knew Jake through her father, pianist Joe Bushkin
20. **Carol Calato** is CEO of Regal Tip Drums
21. **William Clancy** is the author of *Woody Herman: Chronicles of the Herds*
22. **Larry Clothier** has managed Sarah Vaughan, Carmen McRae, Roy Hargrove and Roberta Gambarini.
23. **Lou Colombo** was a world class trumpeter and former baseball player from Cape Cod
24. **Brian Conigliaro** and his father, Joe, were friends of Jake, who was himself a fan of Brian's cousin, Red Sox player Tony Conigliaro
25. **Joe Corsello** is a drummer who worked with Benny Goodman, Peggy Lee and Zoot Sims
26. **Harry Crosby** knew Jake when he worked with his father, Bing
27. **Bill Crow** is a jazz bassist and author who played and laughed with Jake, to his everlasting delight
28. **Jim Czak** is a recording engineer with NoLA Recordings

29. **Elsa Davern** and her clarinetist husband Kenny were good friends of Jake and Denisa's

30. **John DeChristopher** is Vice President, Artist Relations Worldwide for Zildjian Cymbals

31. **Chip Deffaa** is a playwright, director and author of eight books on music and popular culture

32. **Charlie Delaney** is Jake's high school classmate from Dorchester

33. **Ron Della Chiesa** is a Boston radio personality, host of "Strictly Sinatra" and "MusicAmerica," and the voice of the Boston Symphony Orchestra live broadcasts for 20 years

34. **Lennie DeMuzio** got to know just about everyone in music during his 40 years at Zildjian Cymbals

35. **Jim Denham** is a jazz fan and amateur drummer from the UK who admired Jake's work and personality

36. **Frank DeVito** has played the drums with Stan Kenton, Benny Goodman, Woody Herman and Ella Fitzgerald, and toured and recorded with Frank Sinatra and many others

37. **Mat Domber** is President of Arbor Records

38. **Pat Domroese** is a pianist and Jake's mother-in-law

39. **Frank Dorritie** is a performer, arranger, author and Concord Jazz producer from '77 through '86

40. **Terry Douds** is a drummer and recording engineer at WOUB Center for Public Media

41. **Ava DuPree** is a singer/songwriter/ actress from L.A.

42. **Eddie Erickson's** banjo, guitar and vocals serenaded audiences from Disney Land to the banks of the Dordogne; he puts the "E" in BED

43. **Leonard Feather** was a prominent jazz critic and author who wrote *The New Encyclopedia of Jazz*

44. **Joan Filippone** is a childhood friend of Mary Hanna Howard

45. **Vic Firth** was timpanist for the Boston Symphony Orchestra and founded the Vic Firth Company

46. **Med Flory** is a saxophonist, arranger and bandleader who founded Super Sax

47. **Paul Fontaine** attended Berklee with Jake and they both played with Woody Herman

48. **Suezenne Fordham** is a classical jazz fusion pianist who leads the Chamber Jazz LA series

49. **Bob Freedman** is a composer-arranger-musical director-pianist-saxophonist-producer-teacher

50. **Jim Galloway** is a clarinetist and saxophonist who was Artistic Director of the Toronto Jazz Festival

51. **Roberta Gambarini** is a jazz singer who Hank Jones proclaimed the "best new jazz vocalist to come along in fifty years"

52. **Gary Giddins** is a biographer, jazz critic, author, director and long-time writer for The Village Voice

53. **Margaret Glasgow** met Jake through Concord Jazz where she worked for many years

54. **Paul Gormley** is a bass player who worked with Jake over a 35 year period

55. **Danny Gottlieb** is a Grammy Award winning drummer who teaches jazz studies at The University of North Florida

56. **Dave Green** is a bass player who has worked and recorded with many groups in all styles of jazz

57. **Dick Hafer** played saxophone on "The Merv Griffin Show" and with Woody Herman, Benny Goodman and Charles Mingus

58. **Jim Hall** is a jazz guitarist, arranger and composer who has played and recorded extensively

59. **Devra Hall Levy** is a writer and technology expert in music, entertainment and public relations

60. **Jeff Hamilton** is a jazz drummer who has played with Ray Brown, Oscar Peterson and Diana Krall
61. **Scott Hamilton** and his tenor saxophone have played jazz around the world for decades
62. **Denisa Hanna** is a guitarist, bass player, luthier and Jake's wife
63. **Ellen Herdegen** worked for 20 years at the Concord Summer Festival starting Year One: 1969. She met Jake there and looked forward each summer to the music, the parties, the jokes and the *fun*
64. **Dale and Nancy Hibler** are friends of Jake and Denisa's from Southern California
65. **Wally Holmes** is a trumpeter, composer and founder of the Sweet & Hot Jazz Festival
66. **Jack Howard** is Jake's nephew
67. **Joan Howard Fitzgerald** is Jake's niece
68. **Joe Howard** is Jake's nephew and plays the guitar
69. **Mary Hanna Howard** is Jake's sister and sings in perfect harmony
70. **Mimi Howard Zakarian** is Jake's niece and also sings in perfect harmony
71. **Peggy Howard Solari** is Jake's niece
72. **Luther Hughes** is bassist, record producer, music publisher and educator
73. **Nancy Jefferson** is a fan of jazz and of Jake's who she met through her husband, Carl Jefferson.
74. **Andrew Judge** is Jake's nephew and worked in the music business for many years
75. **Brigid Judge** is Jake's niece and a flutist and violinist
76. **Eleanor Hanna Judge** is Jake's sister and can still sing at the drop of a word
77. **Jerome F. Judge** is Jake's nephew and a one-time saxophone player
78. **Paula Judge** is Jake's niece and has been playing the piano since childhood
79. **Rory Judge** is Jake's nephew and has been playing the drums since he was a teenager
80. **Valentina Judge** is Jake's niece
81. **Al Julian** is a music industry executive and promoter, former East Coast representative for Concord Jazz, and Jake's friend for almost 60 years
82. **Anna Julian** and her husband Al were good friends of Jake's
83. **Jerry Kahn's** brother A.J. was Jake's housemate in Los Angeles during the '70s.
84. **Jim Keltner** is a drummer who has played and recorded with a myriad of musicians from the Beatles, to Bob Dylan and Carly Simon
85. **Dave Kenney** is a friend of Jake's from Dorchester
86. **Paul Kenney** is a friend of Jake's from Dorchester
87. **Bev Kennedy** is a friend and fan of Jake's from Sacramento
88. **Stan Keyawa** owns the Professional Drum Shop in Hollywood, one of Jake's favorite hang-outs
89. **Rebecca Kilgore** put the "B" in BED as her jazzy vocals liltingly interpret the great American songbook.
90. **John King** is an author, musician, speaker and teacher
91. **Eiji Kitamura** is a traditional jazz clarinetist from Tokyo who played and recorded with Jake
92. **Bruce Klauber** is a drummer, Gene Krupa biographer and Hudson Music "Jazz Legends" producer
93. **Joe LaBarbera** is a jazz drummer who has worked with Woody Herman, Bill Evans and Chuck Mangione
94. **John LaBarbera** is a cornetist, composer-arranger and Professor of Music at the Univ. of Louisville
95. **Jack LaSpina** was a fellow musician in the Air Force Band

96. **Charlie "The Whale" Lake (Kaljakian)** knew Jake from the time he was Woody Herman's band boy
97. **Terry Lamond** and her drummer husband Don were great friends of Jake's
98. **Jack LeCompte** is a Los Angeles-based drummer and percussionist
99. **Brian Lemon** is a British jazz pianist and arranger who has worked with Benny Goodman, Charlie Watts, and Scott Hamilton
100. **Tom Littlefield** is Woody Herman's grandson and a music industry executive
101. **Joe Locatelli** is a percussionist who knew Jake for more than 50 years
102. **Mundell Lowe** is a jazz guitarist, teacher and composer of music for films and television
103. **Joe Lovano** is a jazz saxophonist, clarinetist, flutist, and drummer.
104. **Bob Macomber** knew Jake from the old neighborhood in Dorchester
105. **Nick Mason** is a drummer who worked as Jake's A&R rep at Regal Tip.
106. **George Masso** is a jazz trombonist, bandleader, vibraphonist and composer specializing in swing
107. **Ken Mathiesson** is a drummer, arranger and founder of the Classic Jazz Orchestra
108. **Jim McCarthy** is a friend of Jake's from Dorchester
109. **Joanne McDermott** is a friend of Mary Hanna Howard's and one of Jake's earliest fans
110. **Doug McKenna** is the son of the great pianist Dave McKenna
111. **Steve McKenna** is the son of the great pianist Dave McKenna
112. **Cheryl McManus** was the Hanna's downstairs neighbor in the three-decker on Washington Street.
113. **Marian McPartland** is the legendary pianist with whom Jake played and recorded
114. **Delores Mello** is a childhood friend of Mary Hanna Howard
115. **Herb Mickman** is a bassist, teacher, pianist and longtime friend of Jake's
116. **Butch Miles** plays drums near Austin, TX. Jake was his friend and drumming hero.
117. **Ed Miller** is a friend of Jake's from Dorchester
118. **Joel Minamide** is a drummer who studied with Jake
119. **Jan Moore** and her husband Bill are friends of Jake's from Vancouver
120. **Mike Moore** is a bassist and member of the Dave Brubeck Quartet.
121. **Gilles Monjeau** is CFO of the Sweet & Hot Jazz Festival
122. **Joe Muranyi** is a jazz clarinetist, producer and critic
123. **Sabine Nagel-Heyer** is CEO of Nagel Heyer Records in Hamburg, Germany
124. **Bill Najjar** is a childhood friend of Jake's from Dorchester
125. **Tal Newhart** is Carl Jefferson's stepson
126. **Roger Neumann** is a saxophone player and bandleader
127. **Gary Novak** is a drummer who has played with George Benson, Chick Corea, and Alanis Morissette
128. **Ruth Nutting** is a childhood friend of Eleanor Hanna Judge
129. **Jack O'Callaghan** is a friend of Jake's from Dorchester
130. **John Oddo** is a pianist, conductor, arranger and musical director who worked with Woody Herman, Rosemary Clooney, Michael Feinstein and Debby Boone, among others
131. **Brian Peerless** organized many of Jake's UK gigs
132. **Bucky Pizzarelli's** jazz guitar has been heard playing with Les Paul, Stephane Grappelli, and Benny Goodman as well as on "The Tonight Show."
133. **Polly Podewell** is a jazz vocalist and friend of Jake and Denisa's

134. **Ed Polcer** is a cornetist who has played jazz since 1950 at festivals, concerts and jazz clubs
135. **Joe Porcaro** is a jazz drummer, percussionist and educator
136. **Doug Ramsey** is a jazz journalist and writer who blogs at Rifftides
137. **John Ratto** is a childhood friend of Jake's from Dorchester
138. **Chuck Redd** is a jazz vibraphonist and drummer who has performed on more than 100 recordings
139. **Randy Reinhart** has played his cornet with Bob Crosby, the Manhattan Rhythm Kings and Vince Giordano's Nighthawks
140. **Michael Rendish** teaches at Berklee College of Music and has composed, orchestrated and conducted 30 film scores
141. **Terrie Richards** is a vocalist and recording artist
142. **Don Robertson** is a drummer who studied with Sonny Igoe
143. **Joe Romersa** is a songwriter, drummer, producer, sound engineer and vocalist
144. **Don and Patti Ross** are friends of Jake's from Los Angeles
145. **Jack Rothstein** has been a jazz fan for 70 years and first met Jake when he was with Anita O'Day
146. **Drew Ruff** is Jake and Denisa's nephew
147. **Jim Rupp** plays and teaches jazz drumming at Ohio State University
148. **Bob Rusch** is a jazz critic and record producer who founded Cadence Magazine and Cadence Jazz
149. **Randy Sandke** has played jazz trumpet for 30 years and was fortunate to work and travel with Jake
150. **Kareem Sanjaghi** is a drummer from Cape Cod who was inspired by Jake
151. **Ray Santisi** is a pianist, Berklee classmate and Berklee faculty member
152. **Manny Selchow** is a producer who organized Jake's tours in Germany
153. **Denny Seiwell** is a drummer who played with Wings
154. **Bill Selditz** organizes the Jake Hanna Drummer Lunches in L.A.
155. **Ed Shaughnessy** is a drummer who played with "The Tonight Show Band"
156. **Fran Shaw** is a childhood friend of Jake's from Dorchester
157. **Jim Shea** is a childhood friend of Jake's from Dorchester
158. **Bobby Shew** is a jazz trumpeter who played with Jake in the Woody Herman band
159. **Robert Louis** Sheehan grew up in Dorchester and taught Modern Languages at Boston College
160. **Dick Sheridan** is a drummer who played, hung out with and attended early morning Mass with Jake
161. **Charlie Shoemake** is a vibraphonist who organizes jazz events in Cambria, Calif.
162. **Richard Simon** is a bass player who was frequently paired with Jake at jazz joints and festivals
163. **Louise Sims** and her husband "Zoot" were great friends of Jake and Denisa's
164. **Hal Smith** is a drummer who has played and recorded extensively
165. **Johnny Smith** is a jazz guitarist, teacher, composer and pilot who loved working with Jake and Bing
166. **Lennie Sogoloff** is a jazz impresario who ran Lennie's on the Turnpike, his club in Peabody, Mass
167. **Rossano Sportiello** is a jazz pianist from Italy who performs internationally
168. **Michael Steinmann** is a writer, videographer and jazz blogger (www.jazzlives.wordpress.com)
169. **Dave Stone** is a bass player who has recorded and performed for film, television and radio

170. **Richard Sullivan** is a jazz fan and Jake fan from Cape Cod
171. **Sunny Sutton** and her husband Ralph were great friends of Jake and Denisa's
172. **Allen Sveridoff** is a musical director and producer who was Rosemary Clooney's longtime manager
173. **Jim Szantor** was the managing editor of Down Beat and editor of the Chicago Tribune
174. **Lew Tabackin** is a saxophonist and co-founder of the Toshiko Akiyoshi-Lew Tabackin Big Band
175. **Scott Thorburn** is a childhood friend of Rory Judge's who adopted Jake as his uncle
176. **Merrilee Trost** knew Jake through Concord Jazz where she was V.P. of Publicity and Promotions
177. **John Tumpak** is a jazz journalist and author of *When Swing Was the King: Personality Profiles of the Big Band Era*
178. **Allan Vaché** is a clarinetist who has performed around the world and recorded extensively
179. **Warren Vaché** is a cornetist, recording artist and good friend of Jake's
180. **Richard Vacca** is the author of *The Boston Jazz Chronicles: Faces, Places and Nightlife 1937–1962*
181. **Johnny Varro** is a jazz pianist, leader and arranger who recorded with Jake
182. **Al Vega** is a pianist who formed the Al Vega Trio in 1950 and kept it going for 61 years
183. **Steve Voce** hosted the BBC Jazz Panorama program and wrote a column for Jazz Journal magazine
184. **Charlie Watts** rocks and rolls for the Rolling Stones and plays some jazz drums
185. **George Wein** is a jazz promoter and producer who founded the Newport Jazz Festival
186. **Clayton White** has been a fan of Jake's since he first heard him play in 1965
187. **Laurie Whitlock** is Assistant Director of the Sweet & Hot Jazz Festival
188. **Roy Williams** is a trombonist who has soloed and all-starred around Europe and the U.S.
189. **Phil Wilson** is a trombonist and Berklee professor who played with Jake
190. **Marshall Wood** is a Boston-area bassist who has worked with Tony Bennett since May 2009
191. **Tom Yeager** met Jake through his father, Bob Yeager, of the Professional Drum Shop
192. **Pete York** is a UK native living in Germany and still playing swinging jazz, his first love

JAKE HANNA DISCOGRAPHY

(A more detailed discography can be found at http://jakehannablog.blogspot.com)

1957 Toshiko Akiyoshi & Leon Sash at Newport
1957 The Many Sides of Toshiko: Toshiko Akiyoshi Trio
1958 Woody Herman and His Orchestra: Live at "Peacock Lane"
1958 A Message from Newport: Maynard Ferguson and his Orchestra
1958 King Porter Stomp
1959 Newport Jazz Festival All Stars
1960 The Spirit Swings Me: Bobby Hackett Quartet
1960 Marian McPartland Plays the Music of Leonard Bernstein

1960	Opus de Jazz, Vol. 2: Johnny Rae Quintet
1961	The most beautiful horn in the world: Bobby Hackett Quintet
1961	Requests on the road: Harry James and His Orchestra
1962	The Woody Herman Quartet
1962	Fourth Herd & the New World of Woody Herman
1962	Dick Ruedebusch with Nat Pierce's Orchestra
1963	Jazz Casual: Woody Herman & The Swinging Herd
1963	Live Guard Sessions: Sarah Vaughan with Woody Herman
1963	The Incredible Kai Winding Trombones
1963	That's Where It Is
1963	Gibbs-Nistico
1964	The Swinging Herman Herd—Recorded Live
1964	Woody Herman-1963 Swingin'est Big Band Ever
1964	Encore: Woody Herman and His Orchestra
1964	Woody Herman: 1963
1964	West Side Story
1965	It's Time We Met
1966	Merv Griffin Presents Mort Lindsey and His Orchestra
1966	Manassas Jazz Festival
1966	Jimmy McPartland: On Stage
1972	Supersax Plays Bird
1973	Seven Come Eleven
1973	Supersax Plays Bird, Vol. 2: Salt Peanuts
1973	Jazz/Concord
1973	Jazz/Concord [Japan]
1973	Concord Jazz Guitar Collection, Vol. 1-2
1974	Supersax plays Bird with strings
1974	Hot & Happy: Bill Berry and the L.A. Band
1974	After You've Gone
1974	Soft Shoe
1975	Supersax: The Japanese Tour
1975	Hot Tracks
1975	Live at Concord: The Hanna/Fontana Band

1975	Rhythm Willie
1975	Barney Plays Kessel
1975	Gems
1975	The Blues
1976	Guitar player: Herb Ellis/Barney Kessel
1976	Father Tom Vaughn's Joyful Jazz
1976	Jake Takes Manhattan
1976	Poor Butterfly
1976	Laurindo Almeida
1976	The King
1976	All Music
1976	All Music [Bonus Tracks]
1976	Kansas City Express
1976	Positively
1976	In Concert
1976	Soaring
1976	On Stage
1976	Chasin' the Bird
1976	Early Autumn
1976	Live at the Concord Summer Festival: Joe Venuti/George Barnes
1976	The 40th Anniversary Carnegie Hall Concert: Woody Herman and The New Thundering Herd
1977	Live from Concord to London
1977	Lost in the Stars
1977	A Tribute to Duke
1977	Scott Hamilton Is a Good Wind Who Is Blowing Us No Ill
1977	Everything's Coming Up Rosie
1977	Soprano Summit Live at Concord
1977	Odessa, Sound of Jazz, Volume 1
1977	100 Years of Recorded Sound
1977	A Tribute to Duke: Nat Pierce Quintet
1978	Cincinnati to L.A.
1978	Rosie Sings Bing
1978	Scott Hamilton 2
1978	Finesse
1978	Sweet Lorraine
1978	Remo Palmier
1978	Soft & Mellow
1978	In Tokyo
1978	Tribute to Billie Holiday
1978	Jillian
1978	First Chair
1978	From This Moment On

1978	Here's to My Lady		1983	Sings the Music of Harold Arlen
1979	Red & Ross		1983	At Toronto's Bourbon Street
1979	No Bass Hit		1983	Symphony
1979	Polished Brass		1983	When You're Smiling
1979	Plays Alto Sax, Flute, Soprano Sax, Clarinet		1983	Stand By for the Jack Sheldon Quartet
1979	Portrait of Marian McPartland		1983	Bye Bye Baby
1979	Herb Ellis at Montreux		1983	No Count
1979	Festival Time		1983	We: Woody Herman/Eiji Kitamura Sextet
1979	Concord Super Band II			
1979	Concord Jazz All-Stars		1984	Indian Summer
1979	Dear friends: Eiji Kitamura with the Concord Jazz All Stars		1984	Jazz Prose: Live at the 1984 Concord Jazz Festival
1979	Horn of Plenty		1984	Swing Low Sweet Clarinet
1979	Marian McPartland At the Festival		1984	Heinie Beau & his Hollywood Sextet
1980	Kansas City 7			
1980	Interplay: Live at the 1980 Concord Jazz Festival		1985	Sings Ballads
			1986	Major League
1980	Scott's Buddy		1986	Tribute to Louis Armstrong and Benny Goodman
1980	Woody Herman Presents, Vol. 1: A Concord Jam		1986	In the swing of things
1980	Woody Herman Presents, Vol. 3: A Great American Evening		1986	Berne, Baby Berne—International Jazz Festival Berne
1980	With Love		1987	Acoustic Live at 3361 Black: Duke Jordan Trio
1980	Swing Eiji			
1980	It Had to Be Us		1987	Compact Jazz: Best of the Big Bands
1981	Apples & Oranges		1988	Supersax: Stone Bird
1981	Firefly		1988	The Jane Jarvis L.A. Quartet
1981	Nonpareil		1988	Woody Herman Memorial: The 40th Anniversary Carnegie Hall Concert
1981	Tour De Force			
1981	Dave McKenna Trio Plays Music of Harry Warren		1988	Swinging into Prominence
1981	Piano Mover: Dave McKenna and the Dick Johnson Reed Section		1989	Jazz at its best: The Legendary Lawson/Haggart Jazz Band
1981	Flat Foot Stampers & Friends. Vol. 1		1989	Leitham Up
			1989	You're the Cats!
1981	Concord Jazz All Stars: At the Northsea Jazz Festival		1990	Concord Jazz: Collector's Series Sampler
1981	Concord Jazz All Stars: At the Northsea Jazz Festival Vol 2		1990	Doug MacDonald Quartet
			1990	In Good Company
1981	Seven Stars		1990	Sweet and Slow
1982	Sings the Music of Cole Porter		1990	30 Jahre Wolverines Jazz Band: Wolverines Jazz Band and their American Friends
1982	Street of Dreams			
1982	Personal Choice			
1982	Too Marvelous for Words: Doc Cheatham & The Hot Jazz Orchestra of New York		1990	Barney Kessel and Friends
			1990	Singin' the Blues
			1991	For the Duration
1982	I've Got a Crush on You: Doc Cheatham with the Hot Jazz Orchestra of New York		1991	Roll Call
			1991	Thirteen Strings
			1991	With a Southern Accent

1991	Retrospective, Vol. 1: Standards
1991	Retrospective, Vol. 2
1991	Groovin' High
1991	Friends in Need: 1991 Triangle Jazz Partyboys
1991	Reminiscin'
1992	Essential Big Bands
1992	Jazz 'Round Midnight: The Big Band
1992	Jubilesta!
1992	Ready—Get Set—Jump
1992	Concord Jazz Guitar Collection, Vol. 3
1992	Crown Royal
1992	Hand-Crafted Swing
1992	You're the Top: Cole Porter in the 1930's
1992	Capitol 50th Anniversary Jazz Box
1992	The Wonderful World of George Gershwin
1993	Concord Jazz Collector's Series Sampler
1993	Great Moments with Ernestine Anderson
1993	Kansas City Nights
1994	Keepin' Time
1994	Prez Impressions
1994	Solos & Duets
1994	Trombone Artistry
1994	Don't You Know I Care?
1994	Flip Phillips: Celebrates his 80th Birthday
1995	Gershwin Songbook: 'S Paradise
1995	Road to Oslo & Play It Again Joe
1995	Complete Gershwin Songbooks
1996	Swing Alive! At the Hollywood Palladium
1996	Verve Jazz Masters 54
1996	Jazz on Bandstand, Vol. 1
1996	Verve Jazz Masters 55
1996	Golden Years
1997	Jerome Kern Songbook
1997	Woody Herman Featuring Stan Getz
1997	Antonio Carlos Jobim Songbook
1997	Cole Porter Songbook
1997	Harold Arlen Songbook
1997	Hoagy Carmichael Songbook
1997	Jerome Kern Songbook

1997	Joint Is Jumpin'
1997	Here's to Zoot
1998	Concord Jazz Heritage Series
1998	Arbors Records Sampler, Vol. 1
1998	Full Circle—Las Vegas Late Night Sessions
1998	Concord Jazz Heritage Series
1998	Saxophone Anthology
1998	Battle of the Bands: Herman Vs. Rich
1998	Benny Carter and the Jazz Giants
1998	Live in 75
1998	Raisin' The Roof: Allan Vache Meets Jim Gallowa
1999	Atlantic/Pacific
1999	1954-1966
1999	Chiaroscuro Songbook, Vol. 1
1999	You're Sensational: Cole Porter in the 20's 40's & 50's
1999	To Bags with Love: A Tribute to Milt Jackson
2000	Live in 75: Japanese Tour, Vol. 2
2000	Swingtime! : Warren Vache & The New York All-Star Big Band
2000	Ballad Essentials
2000	Incontournables
2000	C'Est Magnifique
2000	Songbook Collection
2000	Night Out With Verve
2001	Bill Watrous & Carl Fontana
2001	Ralph Gleason's Jazz Casual [DVD]
2001	Jazz Casual: Woody Herman & The Swinging Herd(CD)
2001	Jazz Casual: Big Bands
2001	Woody Herman's Finest Hour
2001	Jazz Casual: The Swingin' Herd
2001	Christmas in Swingtime
2001	Watch What Happens …
2002	Out of This World
2002	Just Friends
2002	From the Beginning
2002	All-Stars at Bob Haggart's 80th Birthday Party
2002	Double Play: No Bass Hit/Major League
2002	Nagel Heyer Artists: Jazz4Beaches: Music to Enjoy
2002	Tribute to Duke Ellington
2002	Sings Arlen & Berlin

2002	Steppin' Out	2005	Harold Arlen Centennial Celebration
2002	In the Pocket: After You've Gone/ Hot Tracks	2005	Jazz After Dark, Vol. 2 [Playboy]
2002	Best of the Concord Years	2006	Dem's Da Breaks
2003	Arrival: Jazz/Concord/Seven, Come Eleven	2006	Recovered Treasures
		2007	Swing Is Still the King
2003	J.J. Johnson Memorial Album	2007	Cocktails for Two
2003	Concord Records 30th Anniversary	2007	Best of Newport '57: 50th Anniversary Collection
2003	Best of the Concord Years	2008	Woody Herman (Mosaic Select)
2003	Dimensions: A Compendium of the Pablo Years	2008	Sings for Lovers
		2008	1963 Live Guard Sessions
2004	Concord Jazz Sampler Vol.2	2009	Finally Ron
2004	Windows	2009	Hundred Years from Today, Vol. 1
2005	1964		
2005	Ballad Essentials	2009	So In Love
2005	You Brought a New Kind of Love		

Bibliography

Calato, Carol, "Regal Tip CEO Remembers Jake Hanna," Drumhead Magazine, Issue 23, September–October 2010, pp. 92–93.

Clancy, William, *Chronicles of the Herd, New York,* Schirmer Books, 1995, pp. 223–241.

Clooney, Rosemary, and Barthel, Joan, *Girl Singer, An Autobiography,* New York: Doubleday, 1999, pp. 256–257, 261

Cozby, Mrs. Frances G., and Hurley, Miss Frances A., "History of the 761st Air Force Band, 1 October 1951–31 December 1951"

Deffaa, Chip, *In the Mainstream: 18 Portraits in Jazz,* New Jersey: Scarecrow Press, 1992, pp 333–357

Elwood, Philip, Liner Notes to Herb Ellis, Joe Pass, Jake Hanna, and Ray Brown, *Seven Come Eleven,* Concord Jazz, 1973

Feather, Leonard, Rosemary Clooney's Surprise Success, The Los Angeles Times, Apr 6, 1986

Feather, Leonard, Liner Notes to *Live at Concord: The Hanna Fontana Band,* Concord Jazz, 1975

Feather, Leonard, Liner Notes to *Jake Takes Manhattan,* Concord Jazz, 1977

Hanna, Jake, "Education in Jazz," Down Beat, April 19, 1979, p. 6

Hazell, Ed, *Berklee, the First Fifty Years,* Boston: Berklee Press Publications, 1995

Lees, Gene, *Jazz Lives: 100 Portraits in Jazz,* Toronto: McClelland & Stewart Ltd, 1992

Rusch, Bob, "Jake Hanna Interview," Cadence, The Review of Jazz and Blues: Creative Improvised Music, Volume 19, No 5, May 1993, pp. 5–12

Rusch, Bob, "Jake Hanna Interview," Cadence, The Review of Jazz and Blues: Creative Improvised Music, Volume 19, No 6, June 1993, pp. 13–25

Shipton, Alyn, BBC Interview for the Jazz Library, 1995, 1998

Trail, Sinclair, "The Best Seat in the House," Jazz Journal, Vol. 34, No 7, July 1981, pp. 16–17

Tompkins, Les, "In Conversation with Kenny Clare and Jake Hanna," Crescendo International, 1975

Tumpak, John R., *When Swing Was the King: Personality Profiles of the Big Band Era,* Wisconsin: Marquette University Press, 2009, pp 128–131

ABOUT THE AUTHOR

Maria S. Judge's work has been published in *A Cup of Comfort for Breast Cancer Survivors*, Dan Wakefield's *The Story of Your Life*, Peace Corps Online, *The Boston Irish Reporter*, *MIT Tech Talk*, and The Merton Seasonal. A graduate of Holy Cross College and Northeastern University, she served as Associate Dean at the Fletcher School of Law and Diplomacy at Tufts University. She sings soprano in a community chorus, but doubts she ever had the musical chops necessary for her Uncle Jake to accompany her. She lives in the Boston area. Her website is www.mariajudge.com.